THE KNIFE AND THE WOUND IT DEALS

A SHORT STORY COLLECTION

BY

B.E. SCULLY

To Karen!
B.E. Scully
"Bobbi"

FIRBOLG PUBLISHING

www.firbolgpublishing.com

Cover art and design by Ben Baldwin.
http://www.benbaldwin.co.uk/

All photographs public domain

ISBN-13: 978-1478321347
ISBN-10: 1478321342

To the rebels and lovers and dreamers,

the seekers, the searchers, believers…

You know who you are—

and I know you, too.

Verland will transform you...

"This is not written for the young or the light of heart, not for the tranquil species of men whose souls are content with the simple pleasures of family, church, or profession. Rather, I write to those beings like myself whose existence is compounded by a lurid intermingling of the dark and the light; who can judge rationally and think with reason, yet who feel too keenly and churn with too great a passion; who have an incessant longing for happiness and yet are shadowed by a deep and persistent melancholy—those who grasp gratification where they may, but find no lasting comfort for the soul."

Critical acclaim for *Verland: The Transformation*

ForeWord Clarion Review

—First-time author B.E. Scully deftly mixes philosophy, suspense, and humor to create a juicy new twist on the vampire legend. *Verland: The Transformation* is a meditation upon mortality: a thinking reader's vampire novel. Even so, there exists enough creepiness to satisfy people who just love a good scare. Additionally, the author excels at describing settings, and the vivid details about the otherworldly locations add to the overall spookiness of the book. Indeed, the settings themselves become characters, as Scully breathes life into places as diverse as bloody battlefields of Prussia, Mayan villages in the 1930s, and present-day Los Angeles. Each place exudes its own mystical eeriness, which adds to the satisfyingly chilling nature of the novel. Reading *Verland: The Transformation* will forever transform your view of vampires.

Robert Dunbar, author of *The Pines* and *Willy*
—A subtle book, full of quietly tense moments and deeply philosophical themes.

The Kirkus Review
—Scully's debut is a breath of fresh air for the vampire genre. She abandons the popular teenage vampire romance in favor of an old-school gothic approach. Verland's diary overtakes the novel; its elegant style and 19th-century flare provide a noticeable contrast to the main narrative. Perhaps most significantly, as the stories slowly converge, the journal seems more real as Elle's life becomes more fantastical, cleverly fusing timelines without compromising the diary's gothic quality… A perfect blend of contemporary and old-fashioned vampire tales, infused with a bounty of panache.

Peter D. Schwotzer, *Famous Monster of Filmland*

—B.E. Scully pulls out all the stops with this book… Part detective thriller, horror story and one man's (vampire) journey through time, Verland: The Transformation shows that vampire fiction is far from dead in the hands of a great writer… has taken its place alongside such modern vampire classics as Salem's Lot, They Thirst, The Vampire

Hunters, Lost Souls, Carrion Comfort and The Traveling Vampire Show, and also alongside the granddaddy of them all Dracula. It is that good.

Verland: The Transformation is available at Amazon.com and other fine venues. For more of B.E. Scully's short stories, poems, interviews, and other odd scribblings, please visit www.bescully.com

Table of Contents

With Anya's death, William Aughten had lost the only person on earth who understood the unspeakable "Thing" that had haunted his existence and shadowed his soul for over seventy years.

Even more disastrous, he had also lost the only person capable of helping him to keep it at bay.

The priest's voice faded to a hum more suited to the dulled memories of the past than the sharp-edged pain of the present. Will drifted back to the first night he and Anya had spent together, so many years ago now. Any other woman would have walked out of that room and permanently removed his name from her call list. But then again Anya had never been just any other woman.

"I'll go if you want me to," she'd said after an hour of amorous advances had abruptly ended with his declaration that it "sure was getting late."

She buttoned up her blouse, rolled off the bed, and sat down at his desk as if they'd been discussing the weather instead of working each other into an erotic frenzy that would once again come to nothing.

"But I'd rather stay," she added to his complete amazement.

They'd been seeing each other for almost six months, and Will knew that she was more than willing to have sex with him. He hadn't had any intention of telling her why that could never happen. But something about the way she sat there so calm and composed, as if she had been waiting all her life just to learn the truth about Will Aughten, made him blurt out what he'd always sworn to never tell another soul.

"Anya, I like you—in fact, I like you a lot. I think that's obvious enough. But I can never be with you. It's got nothing to do with you personally. It's because of me. Or actually, it's because of what I call the Thing."

In case she wanted to head for the door without a backward glance, Will turned away to indicate that he wouldn't stop her. But she remained sitting there, her clear hazel eyes full of curiosity but still entirely free of judgment.

"Not a very original name, I'll admit," he continued. "But I've never known what else to call it."

"And what is this 'Thing' that causes you to isolate yourself so terribly?" she asked.

"To tell the truth I'm not entirely sure. But it came to me when I was just a little boy—maybe seven, eight years old. I had this vision of a spirit or ghost or *something*. I wasn't asleep, I know that for a fact. And yet it wasn't a human being of flesh and blood. I know that, too." He laughed nervously, still treating it as a joke in case she thought him mad.

"What did the Thing look like?" she asked with perfect earnestness despite his attempts at levity.

"It was an old man—or at least in the shape of an old man. He wore a long gray cloak that covered most of his face and body, but I could see that he was bent over with age and kind of misshapen, as if something was concealed beneath the cloak that caused it to bulge in odd places. I never did get a good look at his face, but somehow I knew he had an expression of such grief that even now I shudder to recall it.

That's what he looked like, in fact—the embodiment of pure and utter grief."

"But was does grief look like?"

"That's just it!" he exclaimed. "That's why to this day I can't describe a single detail about his features. Only the expression... that expression was like a knife-slice straight across my soul."

Anya crossed the room and sat on the edge of the bed. Will's arm was stretched listlessly toward her, but when she reached for his hand he drew it away.

"What did this spirit do that made you so terribly afraid of it?" she asked, her voice tender with concern.

"Oh, it didn't make me afraid of *it*," he said. "It made me afraid of *me*."

By the time Will brushed off the cobwebs of the past, the last of the mourners were trickling away. He stood there as the cemetery workers hedged closer, eager to finish their task but mindful of his presence at the grave. The day was still mild and the skies were clear. He had no one left to visit in the present day world beyond these gates, so he decided to linger with the residents of this one, who were as consigned to the past as he was.

That long ago night he and Anya had talked until the morning sun broke through the faded curtains. He had told her all about the Thing, how without speaking one word it had told him—no, *told* wasn't quite right—it had *revealed* to him the darkest depths of his own twisted, tormented soul. He had always known that he was different. As an infant he had cried for the first year of his life, taking no consolation in his mother's arms. He remained just as singular in adolescence, finding little pleasure in the usual childhood games and failing to make a place for himself among the groups that formed and dissolved and reformed like mysterious schools of fish darting this way and that in instinctual synch with each other.

Will had always felt more like a lone shark in hostile waters, but he'd never quite understood why until the old man had revealed to him the Thing.

It wasn't something that could be defined or even properly named. It was simply something inside of him, some malignant, unimaginable Thing. It slumbered like a serpent in the deepest reaches of his being—and like a deadly serpent, if disturbed or provoked it could lash out and kill anything within striking distance of its poisoned fangs.

His realization of the Thing had been both a relief and a burden. It confirmed the strange, singular destiny he'd always understood as his own. Yet unless he wanted calamity and disaster to darken all the days of his life, it also condemned him to a life of solitude.

Intimacy, for him, was the trip wire that would detonate the land mines buried beneath the surface of his seemingly harmless façade. The grief-ravaged face of the old man was a foreshadowing of all the faces that *he* would create if the Thing were allowed to have its way.

Lying awake after the old man vanished from his darkened room, Will had decided that even though he had been cursed with this Thing, he had at least been warned early enough to prevent its consequences.

Thus, he had told Anya the truth of why he could never allow himself to become close to her or anyone else who might then have to pay the terrible price of the Thing.

She had listened intently without judgment or censure. She seemed to understand the Thing in a way he had not thought possible from someone not afflicted by it. They parted with a bond between them that transcended the usual conventions of courtship. They shared something entirely separate from the trivial concerns and pursuits of most people—they shared the Thing.

Even so, the ordinary business of life marches on. When after a few years Anya took a job in a city halfway across the country, Will was neither surprised nor particularly disappointed. He would miss her company, of course, but in some ways knowing that the Thing remained between them despite their physical separation strengthened the bond even further.

They kept in close touch at first, but eventually their correspondence dwindled and then ceased altogether. Will lost track of Anya and her revolving list of addresses and phone numbers, but she stayed with him nonetheless, a constant reminder that someone else knew the truth about him. Someone else knew about the Thing.

The grief-ravaged face of the old man chaperoned him on every date with every woman who temporarily blinded him to the hazards of his fate. It haunted his dreams with visions of mangled, broken bodies; bruises beneath make-up that never quite concealed their terrible origin; unthinkable transgressions of the flesh and perverse indecencies upon the human form. The Thing spoke to him through every abuser and murderer, every depraved killer who sneered at him from television screens and news headlines—every fool who had dared unleash the Thing.

Unlike those lost souls, Will Aughten had never committed an act of violence in his life. His worst offenses against society were an expired parking meter or occasionally overdue electricity bill. His life was a carefully arranged study of schedules, routines, and unshakeable habits of mind and body. He read the newspaper front to back each morning at breakfast. Once he returned home from work and finished his frugal yet satisfying dinner, he completed the crossword puzzle and went to bed at eleven o'clock each night. He awoke at six-thirty each morning, even on weekends. Will Aughten received numerous accolades and bonuses for never missing a single day of work in his thirty-plus years on the job at Prospect Financial Services.

So when he bumped into Anya May at an art gallery one otherwise ordinary Saturday afternoon, for a moment he didn't quite understand the curious question she asked once they'd completed the obligatory round of "How have you been?"

"So I assume the Thing hasn't yet caught up with you?"

once even went on a day's drive to the coastal towns of the south. Will made a point to take an interest in her life, to discuss subjects other than the Thing. But it was always there between them as if listening for hints of itself behind each of their words, watching for a moment when they'd let their guards down enough for it to slip its chains and break free.

After all, Will never forgot that the one who had done the most to assist him in containing the Thing was also the one most likely to unleash the full force of its violence.

The day was edging toward evening and Will decided to head home. He had started back toward the gate when the overgrown patch of weeds in the far corner of the cemetery caught his eye. He'd walked these shaded lanes hundreds of times, yet he couldn't recall ever seeing this section before.

Curious, he stepped off the cobbled walkway and made his way through the increasingly unkempt grass. There was no lane, and apparently no one had been assigned to clear the hawthorn bushes and snaking ivy vines that grabbed his ankles and clawed at his pants.

Will soon realized why this part of the cemetery was so overgrown. Although there were two or three dozen graves scattered about, they all appeared to be long abandoned. Some of the graves had sunken with time, the weathered headstones stained green with moss and mildew. Many of the once beloved names were now blackened with neglect.

The most dismal, depressing of places could not have outdone this weed-choked monument to dereliction and decay.

It felt even chillier in this forsaken corner where the shadows seemed to stretch from the over-hanging trees like desperate, grasping arms. Driven by some morbid curiosity, Will leaned down and inspected one of the headstones. The worn inscription was difficult to read, but he could make out the numbers marking the duration of the poor soul's life—only a few short years between the time of birth and the time of death.

He scanned a few more of the headstones. The graves ranged from the early 1900s to the present day, but all bore the same distressing pattern in regard to the dates recording their inhabitants' time on earth—all of the headstones bore dates marking a timespan of mere years or months. Or even, in some sad cases, a scant few days.

Had he stumbled upon some children's graveyard? But why was it so forgotten and overgrown despite graves as fresh as one month's time?

A lonely tomb along the farthest edge caught his eye. It was white, newer than the rest. Even though the first bruises of twilight had begun to darken the sky, Will felt drawn toward the little headstone tilting sideways as if searching for some lost companion. He noticed that the earth was still dark as if only recently overturned.

As he drew nearer to the grave, Will was suddenly seized with a dread so intense that he almost turned and fled—almost, but something even more powerful than his fear drove him to his knees in front of the inscription that he already knew would bear his name. The dates beneath made the shock of actually seeing it all the more profound:

William N. Aughten

April 1st, 2012—April 1st, 2012

It was a date already imprinted upon his soul as certainly as it was now carved into this cursed tomb, for it marked the day of the last time he had seen Anya May alive.

Of course he'd noticed throughout the previous winter that she'd begun to move much slower, that she rarely had strength enough for their walks at the river. But they were both getting older, after all, and this thought comforted him until he stopped by her house that afternoon on the first day of April.

She was resting in her favorite chair by the bay window, covered by a thick blanket despite the warmth of the room. The sunlight streaming through the glass lit up her paper-thin skin as if it were translucent. For a moment he felt as if he were gazing at a heavenly angel just landed on earth rather than a flesh and blood human being.

Taken aback by her frail appearance, he hesitated in the doorway, but she beckoned him in with her usual smile. Drawing his own chair closer, Will noticed that despite the condition of her body, the clear hazel eyes were exactly the same as they'd always been.

"Anya, you are not well today," he said. Despite his disgust at his selfishness, he couldn't hold back a twinge of annoyance at her illness. If she left him now, how would he ever contain the Thing? Far from growing weaker with time, it only seemed to become stronger and more determined in proportion to his own decline. Would the Thing finally overtake him at the end, without Anya there to help him?

If she sensed any irritation on his part, she was too gracious to let it show. "I am not well most days, I'm afraid. I expect that I will not be greeting too many more spring afternoons, my friend."

"Oh, Anya, don't say that! How would I ever manage without you?" In light of her sickly condition, Will was reluctant to reference the Thing in case it might upset or excite her. But she herself brought up the one subject that had always loomed largest between them.

"You needn't worry yourself about the Thing anymore, at least," she told him.

He'd always felt that in some ways Anya understood the Thing even more instinctively than he did. If she felt that it was no longer a threat, then it must have been vanquished somehow. But why did he still feel that paralyzing dread, that sense of certain impending catastrophe and doom?

"And so it is no longer with me?" he asked.

She reached out to take his hand. He had always avoided physical contact with her as much as possible. Why lure the Thing out of its hiding place with a temptation such as that? But of course that didn't matter now. Soon Anya would be in a place where not even his darkest impulses could harm her.

Yet he still hesitated. After denying himself the pleasure of intimacy for so long, the thought of taking her hand now seemed impossible, even disagreeable. It was as if the fading warmth of her skin against his own, the dimming pulse in her veins alongside his still-strong one would somehow pull him toward the grave along with her.

Pretending he needed to stretch his legs, he rose from his chair and stepped out of her reach. With great difficulty, she stood and reached out for him again. A part of him wanted more than anything in the world to take her hand, to hold her in his arms at last despite the cursed Thing!

But he could not do it. He shrank away and tucked his hands into the safety of his coat pockets. She sank back onto her chair, and the last of the life seemed to drain from her body. Even her eyes looked clouded and dull for the first time since he'd known her.

Will mumbled his excuses and left without even saying a proper goodbye. He had wandered the streets half the night in a frenzy of confusion and guilt, and then returned to her house the next morning as early as propriety would allow.

He had to know if the Thing had been vanquished, if he was free at last from its clutches!

But her housekeeper told him that Anya was too ill to receive visitors. Later that day he received the telephone call informing him of her death.

He'd stood there with his calendar scribbling down the bewildering flurry of memorial services to follow. That's when he'd taken note of the date of their final meeting—a particularly cruel April Fool's Day indeed.

A shadow not emanating from the trees fell across Will Aughten's bent and trembling shoulders. He hadn't noticed the intruder's approach, but when he struggled to his feet and turned to face him he immediately recognized the grey woolen cloak and the stooped, misshapen form it concealed.

He stepped back, clutching one hand over his wildly pounding heart and pointing at the tombstone with the other. "What is the meaning of this place?"

"This place is what it appears to be," the old man replied.

"But what is the meaning of these birth and death dates so close together?"

"The dates on these stones do not mark the time on earth of those now beneath it. They mark the time in each of their lives when they could have chosen to truly live, but instead chose to remain in the shadow of death that eventually led them here."

A vision of Anya May rose before Will's eyes. He reached out to her, but she flickered away from him and disappeared.

"Anya!" He turned to the old man in helpless rage. "This tomb that bears my name—these dates upon it!"

"That is the day you almost allowed yourself to love another and to accept love in return."

The old man reached up and pulled back the hood of his cloak. Will Aughten stared into his own face, as grief-ravaged now as the prophecy had promised it would be. He saw the Thing fully revealed for what it was, for what it had always been—*his* creation, *his* self-prophecy—his own grief fulfilled.

William N. Aughten finally understood that *he* was both the Thing and its consequence.

He stumbled backward and gripped his heart. The tangled ivy caught his feet and tripped him into the rectangle of fresh earth at the foot of the tombstone that bore not just his name but his fate.

The dates stared down at him like empty, mocking eyes.

They were the last things he saw as his heart gave up the struggle to live that had begun too late and been given too little.

There weren't many mourners at William Aughten's funeral—a handful of coworkers from Prospect Financial Services; a few fourth cousins once removed whose heads were already full of whatever useless trinkets and trifles they could seize from his no doubt meager estate. Everyone agreed that it was touching that the old gentleman had arranged to be buried next to the one person who had meant something in his otherwise lonely life—his old friend Anya May.

"And to think they found him dead of a heart attack right there on the grave where they'd just buried her not hours before!"

"Strange… guess some people just can't live without each other."

"I always wondered why they never got married. She was always so fond of him."

"At least they'll be together now," they all agreed as the shovelfuls of earth began to cover the casket.

The mourners sighed and shook their heads, then trickled away to let the cemetery workers complete their grim task.

An old man no one had recognized was the last to linger by the grave. He wore a long gray cloak that covered most of his face and his bent, oddly misshapen form.

None of Will's far-flung relatives or handful of acquaintances had understood the meaning of the epitaph chosen for his headstone. But since it had already been ordered and paid for by the time the funeral arrangements were complete, no one had objected to the oddness of the inscription. The grave would no doubt soon be forgotten anyway, they reasoned, its resident and his final words both eroded by time.

At least one mourner, however, had not yet begun to forget. The old man kneeled at the tomb and ran his withered fingers over each of the etchings as if memorizing their message for an eternity of tombs yet to come:

William N. Aughten

October 22, 1940—April 7, 2012

This Thing Lives Because He Would Not

Champ's Last Round

"If anybody would return from the grave to take revenge on those who put him there, it's the Champ," the Professor said. "I'm telling you, all of us are just walking dead men at this point."

The four men mopping the gymnasium floor with the Professor had varying reactions to their new status.

Rufus banged the side of his head in order to adjust the receptor that received secrets messages from the Agency that had implanted it in his brain years ago. Fisk started sputtering like a kettle of boiling water, and K.C. sat in silent communion with the beings that lived on the planet as yet undiscovered by any other person on this one. Hard-Top seemed pissed off, but then again Hard-Top always seemed pissed off, which is why he'd ended up in The Cutt in the first place.

It was officially known as The Vandercutt Psychiatric Institute for the Criminally Insane, but everybody just called it The Cutt.

"Couldn't pick a better name for it," Hard-Top always said. "You cut somebody *up*, they cut you *out* by sending you here. Nothin' *but* cuttin' 'round this place."

"Quite *ironical*," the Professor added, consulting the pocket-sized Dictionary he always carried.

None of them had wanted to cut down the Champ, though. He was from the old school time when fighters came up from the mean streets and stayed that way even once the money started rolling in.

"Fighters nowadays are like rock stars with their agents and publicity teams," Champ used to say. "Put me in a ring and I'll show you what them Tomato Can Sams are made of."

Champ hadn't been back in the ring, though, ever since he'd delivered a K.O. punch that sent some poor sucker on an early trip to the Promise Land. The problem was that he hadn't been anywhere near a boxing ring when he'd done it. Champ had been waiting for his wiener to boil at a hot dog stand on Tenth Street when the guy behind the counter banged down a pair of metal tongs. For some reason that had sent Champ to thinking the fight bell had gone off, and he delivered a one-two punch that ensured that dude had sold his last dog.

After that the Champ got to hearing that fight bell more and more—anything from construction work to a door clanging shut could start Champ throwing punches at anybody close enough to end up his unlucky opponent. A new orderly who hadn't yet learned the score on Champ had once slammed down a metal tray in the day room, and Champ had hit him so hard he'd knocked three teeth loose. It had taken four guards to take the Champ down that day, and he'd done a tidy little stretch in solitary for it.

Not even Dr. Rooker could tame the Champ, and he was supposed to be the expert in treating what he called "chronically anti-social personality disorders." He'd won all kinds of awards and had a big-deal job at some university before he'd ended up at The Cutt. Nobody could figure out what had made a hot-shot like Rooker trade all that for a gig pushing pills and writing reports nobody would read about a bunch of criminally insane psychopaths.

"I'm in the business of helping people, and who needs more help than the men who have ended up here?" he'd say.

That's how all of the inmates knew to watch their backs around Rooker—there never was a person could do more harm than the kind hell-bent on saving everyone else from it.

Most of the inmates at The Cutt were too zombied out on the fistfuls of psychoactive drugs they took like clockwork three times a day to be much harm to anybody anymore. But there were always what Dr. Rooker called those "chronically anti-social personalities" that just couldn't seem to get along.

The Champ was a top-notch example of one of those personalities.

Even the guards respected the fact that even in a shithole like The Cutt, the Champ still carried himself like the ten-to-one winner he'd once been. Nobody messed with the Champ, and for other chronically anti-social personalities like the Professor, Fisk, Hard-Top, K.C., and Rufus, he would always be the Champ even if he never stepped into another ring.

So out in the yard that day on clean-up duty, killing him had been the last thing on any of their minds. Everyone was just joking around and complaining like usual when the bucket slipped out of K.C.'s hand and went clattering to the concrete like the heavens themselves had rung that fight bell.

Even K.C. had come down to earth on that one. He'd looked over at the Champ with the sheer terror of what he knew was coming.

By the time the rest of them descended like a pack of scared rabbits on a wild grizzly bear, the Champ had delivered a hard upper cut to K.C.'s jaw and was going at his liver like a battering ram.

Hard-Top cracked him a good one with the business end of a broomstick, but it didn't even slow him down. Rufus swung the bucket against the side of his head and the Professor started banging on his skull with a mop. Fisk, armed only with a big yellow scrubbing sponge, tossed that aside in favor of his fists.

None of which seemed to be doing a lick of good until the Champ suddenly went dead still and stood there with his eyes as empty as two knot holes in a fence. Then just like a big oak tree finally cut deep enough to be brought down, the Champ slowly timbered forward and hit the ground with a mighty thud.

The Professor was the first to move. He felt for vitals and put his hand in front of the Champ's mouth to check for breath. Finally he shook his head and said, "He seems to have expired."

"We killed the *Champ?*" Fisk said. A fire bug from the first time he'd watched his mother light the burners on the kitchen stove, Fisk had burned half of himself up along with the warehouse he'd set ablaze on his last arson run, and whenever he got nervous the left side of his face went all quivery like a pool of molten lava.

"Self-defense," Rufus said, adjusting his receptor. "According to the Agency such actions are justified in cases where the threat of bodily harm is present."

But Hard-Top was already gathering up the brooms and buckets. "Tell that to my next life sentence. No way am I goin' down for this one. No way."

They all stared down at the massive lump of destroyed human flesh.

"Everyone knows who was on the work detail," Fisk said.

Hard-Top shoved a mop into his hands. "That don't prove nothin'. Let's clear out and go to chow as usual. We can say we left the Champ out here to finish up and that's the last we saw of him."

"The plan might have *feasibility*," the Professor weighed in. "After all, the Champ did have quite a few unwilling boxing partners with scores to settle."

"Right," Hard-Top said. "Everybody swear to secrecy right here, right now."

Each one of them swore on their graves to keep the secret. K.C., who never spoke a word even when his jaw wasn't swelling shut, nodded his consent and the pact was sealed.

The guards eventually found the Champ after he failed to show up for his round of dinner meds. An investigation was launched, but nobody poked around all that long or hard. The Champ didn't have anybody on the outside who cared if he was alive or dead, and more than a few were relieved to hear it was the latter. His murder was filed under "Unsolved" along with a hundred others, and that's where it would have stayed if a month later the Professor hadn't seen the Champ standing in the shower room looking as mean and nasty as any ghoul come back from the grave with a score to settle.

"Are you sure it was the Champ?" Fisk asked when they all met up in the day room to discuss the situation.

"One hundred-and-ten perfect, *unequivocally* sure," the Professor said. He was an obsessive-compulsive who had lost it one day and almost killed his wife for putting his tea cup back in the cupboard the wrong way, so he knew a thing or two about details.

The left side of Fisk's face was twitching like Mount Vesuvius ready to blow. "Maybe it was just somebody who looks like the Champ."

"Nobody on either side of the grave looks like the Champ," Hard-Top said. "Tell us again what happened, Prof."

"Like I said, I was the only one left in the shower room. You know how I prefer my privacy in such matters. I had just turned on the water when I turned around and saw the Champ crouched against the wall by the towel racks. He was thinner and more sickly looking than when he was alive, and his eyes were all blood-shot and rolling around in their sockets. But it was *definitely* the Champ. Same scar on his forehead and everything."

"But you didn't go up to him?"

"No. I pissed myself right there on the floor and screamed my bloody lungs out," the Professor said. "If you'll excuse my lack of eloquence."

"And by the time the guards showed up the Champ was gone," Rufus said, banging the side of his head. "I've reported that part of the incident to the Agency, but so far they haven't gotten back to me with a possible explanation."

"The explanation is that we killed him and now he's come back to take revenge," the Professor said. "We're walking dead men, I tell you."

"The Champ never let anybody put him on the ropes when he was alive," Fisk said. "I guess it stands to reason he'd come back from the dead for one last round."

Hard-Top banged his fist against the table and stood up. "I don't believe in no ghosts. There are enough live bastards in this place who want to kill a man without worryin' about some dead one tryin' to do the job."

He stomped out of the day room and the meeting was adjourned. But that night all four men slept with one hand on whatever weapon they had hidden beneath their mattresses, and the next morning not even the Professor lingered in the shower room.

K.C. was the first to turn up missing. If he wasn't on a work detail he was usually in his cell conversing with the voices in his head, so when he didn't show up for his P.M. meds no one was overly concerned. But when the guards checked his cell all they found was a puddle of blood big enough to satisfy even Count Dracula's worst cravings. They searched every cell on every floor and combed every inch of the grounds, but his body was never found.

A week later Rufus went into a padded room in solitary after the Agency told him to bite a guard on the thumb and didn't come back out. His body never turned up, either.

By then Fisk was a walking basket case, so when he came tearing into the day room one afternoon shaking so badly he could hardly keep himself on a chair, no one paid any attention. But they paid attention quick enough when he claimed to have just seen the Champ on the second floor sick ward where Fisk had been on janitorial duty.

"It was just like the Professor said," Fisk told them. "The Champ looked like a monster from some horror movie, skin kind of green and eyes like a mad dog or somethin'. But the worst part is that he *saw* me, man—he looked straight at me, pointed his finger, and started moaning just like a damn zombie or somethin'!"

"Calm the hell down!" Hard-Top shouted in a tone guaranteed not to calm Fisk down.

"What happened then?" the Professor asked.

"I was scared too shitless to even scream. The Champ started comin' toward me and I'd be a goner right now if some nurse wouldn't have poked her head around the corner just in time."

Hard-Top banged his fist on the table. "What does some nurse have to do with anything?"

"I don't know, but as soon as she showed up, the Champ disappeared," Fisk said.

"It appears as if the Champ can only materialize when no one else is present but his intended victim," the Professor said. "So we're safe as long as we're never alone."

With that in mind, the three remaining men became the most sociable inmates in The Cutt.

A few uneventful weeks went by, then a month. They began to think that maybe the Champ had finally laid himself to rest—until Fisk went missing in the yard one day and was never seen again alive *or* dead.

Even the guards started watching their backs once word got around that the Champ had come back to take revenge against anyone who had done him wrong. When the time came for Hard-Top's monthly check-in with Dr. Rooker, the subject was one of the first things to come out of the good doctor's mouth.

"I'd like to get a sense of what's going on with all of these rumors lately about inmates coming back from the dead and killing people."

"Sense is people are scared," Hard-Top said.

"But ghosts don't kill people, Mr. Harden. *People* kill people." The doctor opened a file on his desk and started leafing through the pages as if he hadn't already seen them a hundred times before. "Delusional paranoia manifesting in aggression toward others. Seems you were sent to Vandercutt for attacking your neighbor after you became convinced that he'd sent his cat into your yard to spy on you."

"Some people shouldn't own cats."

"And some people shouldn't hold imaginary grudges, eh, Mr. Harden? I find it interesting that you are associated with all of the inmates who have gone missing lately."

Hard-Top might not have been smart like the Professor, but he could smell a dirty rotten set-up from a mile away. "I didn't have nothing to do with it."

"No," Dr. Rooker said, closing the file. "I'm sure you never do. But rest assured that from now on we're going to be keeping a much closer eye on things around here. Please keep that in mind, Mr. Harden."

That afternoon Hard-Top called an emergency meeting with the Professor in the day room. They were the last of the Champ's murderers left alive.

"We can't just stroll up to the warden and ask for protection," Hard-Top said. "I mean, 'Hey, we bashed the Champ to death and now he's come back for revenge' isn't going to do us no favors."

"I have been *cogitating* the matter ever since K.C. vanished," the Professor said. "And I have come to the conclusion that the only way out is to get out—literally."

"How do you mean?"

The Professor looked around to make sure that no one was watching. He pulled a carefully folded up piece of paper from the pages of his Dictionary and spread it on the table in front of him.

"This is an original building plan for The Vandercutt. I tore it out of a very interesting book I discovered in the library. When The Cutt was built in the early nineteen-hundreds, it was an asylum for ordinary crazy people. Only later did they decide to lock it down for us criminally inclined ones."

"What's your point, Prof?"

"*This* is my point," the Professor said, pointing to a section of the building plan. "This is a tunnel that runs underneath the main building. They used it to get from one place to another without having to go through each of the wards and continually disturb the patients. Quite ingenious, really. Rumor had it that there was a secret room down there where they kept the most violent inmates. Anyway, the tunnel still exists, but most of the doors were sealed up years ago and all of them are now pad-locked shut. But it just so happens that one of the unsealed doors is at the back of a closet in the emergency care room of the second floor sick ward. And the tunnel it connects to just so happens to lead to a very quiet corner of the east wing that would be most uninhabited late at night."

"So if we get ourselves into the sick ward and break the lock in the closet, then what? How do we get out the east wing door if it's locked from the outside?"

"They don't call me the Professor for nothing, my dear man. A nicely bribed caretaker has already removed the outside lock on the east wing door, and yours truly made sure that the lock on the closet door is hanging just a little more loosely than it was a day ago."

In order to avoid suspicion, they spaced their health complaints a few days apart. Hard-Top went first, but when four days went by and the Professor still hadn't shown up in the sick ward, he started to get worried.

Eventually, he brought it up with one of the nurses. "I thought the old goat would at least stop by to visit."

"Oh, I'm sorry to have to tell you this," she told him anyway. "But your friend has been missing for three days now. He was in the shower room by himself one morning and just disappeared without a trace."

No one would ever call Hard-Top a cowardly man, but he had to force his voice steady long enough to ask the one thing he needed to know. "Did anybody find that little Dictionary he always had with him? It probably sounds stupid, but a man doesn't make many friends in a place like this, so to have something of his to keep with me…"

Hard-Top had never once cried in all of his life, but he didn't need to manufacture the tears in his eyes at the thought of that lost blueprint.

Luckily the nurse had a soft spot and the next day she brought him the Dictionary. After lights-out, Hard-Top carefully flipped through the pages. The folded up piece of paper was tucked into the "E" words—the first entry at the top of the page was "Escape."

Hard-Top wasn't going to wait around any longer for the Champ to come for him. If he was ever going to make it out of The Cutt, it would have to be tonight.

He waited until the orderly started his rounds and then slipped out of bed. The closet in the emergency care room was along the far side of the wall. After pushing aside some boxes of medical supplies, Hard-Top found the tunnel door.

The lock was hanging loose just like the Professor said it would be.

Before squeezing through the uncomfortably small doorway, Hard-Top ducked back into the room. The drawers beneath the exam table were locked, but it didn't take much to pry them open. In the bottom drawer he found what he was looking for—a razor-sharp scalpel that he tucked into the extra fold at the bottom of his pant leg.

It might be impossible to kill a ghost, but maybe he could slow one down long enough to make it to that east wing door.

The steep stairway was pitch black and Hard-Top had to go slow to keep from stumbling. If the tunnel was this dark, he might never find his way through. But when he reached the bottom of the stairs the tunnel was well-lit by a string of emergency lights running along the ceiling. Why would anybody need lights down here if it had been sealed up for decades?

Hard-Top decided to leave that question for another day. He started through the tunnel as fast as he could go without getting lost. It was a maze of snaking corridors and he had to check the blueprint frequently to make sure he was headed toward the right door. He was halfway through the central part of the building when he saw something that stopped him cold in his tracks.

An old rocking chair had been left in the tunnel by some long-ago orderlies who probably sneaked down here for an afternoon nap. Even though those orderlies were long dead by now, the chair was rocking back and forth as if one of them had just jumped into action after being caught snoozing on the job.

When a low moan came from somewhere behind him, Hard-Top had to force his legs not to buckle right out from under him.

He turned around and there was the Champ—or at least some version of what the Champ used to be. This Champ was as unwholesome looking as the Professor and Fisk had said he was. His already battered face was now blotched with mossy green patches and his skin hung off him in lifeless folds.

As the Champ began to drag toward him, Hard-Top leaned down and retrieved the scalpel from his pant leg. "Come and get me, big guy."

The Champ was now moaning to beat the band and pointing at Hard-Top as if to say, "You did it!" Hard-Top waited until the Champ was almost on him before driving the scalpel into the side of the Champ's neck.

The big guy fell to his knees, then reached up and pulled the scalpel out of his neck. It started spouting like a fountain, and Hard-Top wondered why a ghost would bleed.

"Yoooouu… kiiiiiillled… meeee!" the Champ moaned, looking up at Hard-Top in utter surprise.

"It was an accident!" Hard-Top yelled back.

The Champ struggled out of his shirt, wadded it into a ball, and pressed it against his leaking neck. All of a sudden it occurred to Hard-Top that maybe the Professor hadn't been as smart as he thought he was. Maybe he hadn't been able to tell the difference between a dead body and a knocked-cold one.

"We thought we killed you that day in the yard!" Hard-Top said, sinking to his knees beside the Champ. "We thought you'd come back from the dead to murder us all!"

"Not muuuurder you… *waaaaarn* you!" the Champ clarified, pointing his finger again before toppling face forward to the floor. Only this time Hard-Top realized that *he* wasn't the one the Champ had been pointing at.

It was a realization that came too late to prevent the sharp blow to the back of his head that left him too dazed to fight off the hands now dragging him to a room at the far end of one of the snaking corridors.

Hard-Top figured those rumors about a secret room were true after all.

A man in a lab coat was laying out a nasty-looking spread of medical instruments on a gleaming metal tray. He turned around and gave Hard-Top a smile as nasty as the tools of his trade.

"Welcome to my laboratory," Dr. Rooker said. "As you can see, your friends have already joined me."

He gestured to a line of hospital beds. Strapped into the first four were K.C., Rufus, Fisk, and the Professor. Hard-Top already knew who would fill the fifth.

The guards still holding each of his arms hustled him over to the bed and strapped him down. Two more came in struggling under the weight of the Champ's body, still massive even despite the starvation diet.

"Put him on that table over there," Dr. Rooker said. He examined the body and then covered it with a sheet. "I don't think he'll be troubling us any longer."

Doctor Rooker dismissed the guards and they left the room without a word between them. Hard-Top wondered how much extra was in *their* paychecks each month, not just for the overtime but to keep their mouths good and shut.

"Such a shame about your friend—the 'Champ,' as I believe you called him," Dr. Rooker said. "What a fine specimen, too! The first round of experiments was going so well, and then he somehow managed to escape. He always was such a *stubborn* one! I have no idea how he evaded us this long—and then popping up to scare the daylights out of people upstairs! But luckily you've helped to eliminate that little problem. And as it turns out, those silly rumors about a murderous ghost came in quite handy in procuring even *more* specimens."

"What the hell did you do to them?" Hard-Top yelled even though he already knew the answer. Dr. Rooker was a big-shot in his field, but even big shots had to obey the law. It was much easier to find human lab rats to experiment on in a place like Vandercutt than in some fancy university. All of a sudden it made all kinds of sense why the good doctor had traded one for the other.

"You see, one of my profession's most crucial tasks is to treat society's chronically anti-social personalities," Dr. Rooker said. "However, in my opinion we have thus far been much too conservative in doing so."

The doctor walked back over to the tray and began arranging the medical instruments. Each time he picked one up and brought it down against the tray it made a metallic clang—a sound like a bell might make calling fighters into the ring.

Out of long habit, Hard-Top glanced over at the Champ. That blow to the head must have really messed him up, because Hard-Top could have sworn he saw the Champ's huge hands clench into fists beneath the crumpled white sheet.

Maybe the Professor couldn't tell the difference between a dead body and a knocked-cold one, but Hard-Top figured a bona-fide medical doctor sure as hell should be able to.

The medical instruments were still clanging away as Hard-Top watched the sheet fall to floor as the Champ rose up from the table.

"You see, psychoactive drugs are only the beginning," Dr. Rooker was saying. "We haven't even begun to explore the possibilities of genetic engineering, neural manipulation… even some modified version of the frontal lobe lobotomy, which has unfortunately been much maligned—"

But the good doctor never got a chance to finish that thought. Instead he got his own modified version of the frontal lobe lobotomy, perfected and performed by the Champ, who had come in off the ropes for one last round.

Blueprints for The Vandercutt Institute for the Mentally Deranged

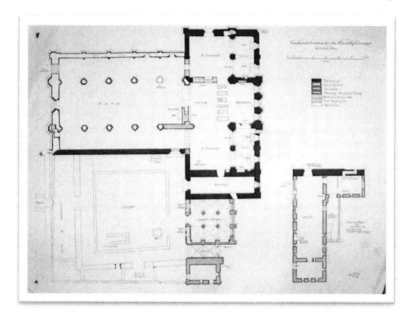

"Rumor had it that there was a secret room down
there where they kept the most violent inmates..."

Animal Undertaking

The opossum was splayed on its back with its legs in the air like an overturned lawn ornament. Its rib cage was split in half and a sticky-looking string of innards was strung across the ditch. I figured it had been dead less than three, maybe four hours. Definitely still in the fresh stage, though not for much longer with the temperature already eighty-five degrees and not even afternoon yet.

I snapped a picture and recorded the exact time and place for later on. It was kind of a milestone, I guess. That opossum was my hundredth road kill spotting. Maybe there'd be some kind of prize— maybe it would even be the phone.

The phone had been the first thing to go wrong between me and Grandma that summer. Usually I got along better with Grandma than anybody else in the world, and she knew I'd do just about anything for her. But it can get kind of hard with old people, them not keeping up with the things a young person needs to get by.

"We didn't have telephones or televisions in my day, let alone these computer shenanigans," she'd tell anybody who'd listen and some that wouldn't. "When I was a girl, most people in Cheat Lake didn't even have running water or electricity. Had to fetch water from the well morning, noon, and night, plus do your business out of doors in all kinds of weather. And now my own grandson says he needs a phone he can carry around with him and send messages to people he's never even seen the flesh of and who knows what-all else."

It was true we didn't have an extra dollar to waste at the end of a month, but when you've never had much of anything, sometimes a thing you can't get starts to seem like a whole lot of something even if it ain't. I guess that's how it was with me and that phone.

"I'll earn some money to pay for it," I promised.

"Then you'd be the first Ottershaw to pay for anything around here in I don't know how long."

Which wasn't exactly true, but wasn't exactly not true, either.

There'd been plenty enough money when Mama was still alive on account of her having the touch. She could just put her hands on someone's knotted up legs or upset stomach and start moving them around and making circle motions, and just like that they'd start feeling better. People used to drive from as far away as Charleston just to have Mama put the touch on them.

She was a healer, Momma was, but it turns out she couldn't put the touch on herself when the cancer came. The doctors at the hospital weren't much better at it for all their big words and fancy treatments. They tried every trick in the book just like Mama had, but sometimes a thing is just too big for one body to handle.

Money used to come in from my pop and Grandpa, too, but unlike Mama they didn't have to do much work to earn theirs. All they had to do was stand around looking like what the rest of the world thought a genuine hillbilly should look like. They both had the same hawk beak noses, hatchet cheeks, and heads full of grizzled hair that were only outdone by their bird's nest beards. I'd been told the

Ottershaws had Cherokee blood in them, but all I knew of the family were a bunch of Irish moonshiners from way back when West Virginia was even wilder than it is now. Anyway, I lost count of how many times I'd seen Papa or Grandpa or sometimes both together on the cover of some tourist guide or one of those plaques with sayings on them that you see in truck stops and souvenir stands. Sometimes even big deal artists from as far away as New York City came to copy their faces for paintings or take photographs of them standing around looking solemn.

For all I know, to this day they're both hanging in museums and galleries all over the world in places I've never even heard about. We once lived for half a year off the money Grandpa got from a line of greeting cards, and all he had to do was sit around in bib overalls smoking this silly corn cob pipe like you'd never really see anyone do in real life. Smoking the corn cob pipe, I mean, not wearing the bib overalls. I'll admit there are a lot of those around Owl Creek County.

Grandma always said it was some kind of world that would paint a picture of a man because he looked like a hillbilly and then not allow him inside the places that sold it for the exact same reason. Grandma could be kind of cranky like that, but you can bet she spent the money just the same.

Then Papa got killed in a boating accident and Grandpa got the sugar disease that took a little bit more of him away each year so that finally there wasn't nothing left to take. Now it was just Grandma and me. She was too old to work and I didn't get neither the touch nor the hatchet cheekbones, but we got by just the same. Not enough for that phone, though, and that's pretty much how I got started on the whole road kill thing.

Seems too many folks had been colliding with wildlife around Cheat Lake, so some government person decided to start tracking road kills during the summer tourist season in order to identify trouble spots and cut down on accidents. They figured the tourists would be a whole lot happier that way, and I figured the poor critters would be even happier.

That's how I came across the flyers in all the gas stations and grocery stores asking for volunteers to search around for road kill and then enter a record in a big online database. They wanted the location, a description of the wildlife, and a photo. All you needed was a car to get around, and since my Uncle Johnny said I could borrow his as long as I helped him fix up his wood shed before winter, I was all set to hunt myself some flattened hide. The work didn't pay nothing, but the thing I was interested in was that all volunteers got a phone with all the bells and whistles needed for the job. The best part was all usage charges were covered by Uncle Sam.

"You'd think the government would have better things to do with people's hard-earned money than have fools searchin' around the roads for dead things," Grandma snorted. But I got my phone and she got me out of the house for the summer, so everything was working out just fine.

Until Grandma started getting sick, that is.

"I'm not going to no hospital and I'm not going to no cemetery, either," she told me after her cough kept getting worse even after Old Man Grady had tried all his remedies. "Everyone I know is dead already, so why should I stick around all by myself?"

"I ain't dead," I'd remind her.

"No, but one of these days you'll fall crazy heels in love and the two of you young fools will run off and get married. I won't see neither one of ya till the love wears down to normal, by which time I'll be long gone from this world."

"Not me, Grams. I ain't the marrying kind," I'd always say.

It was true, too. As far as most folks were concerned, I was like a clock with no hands on it—keeping time just fine on the inside, but pretty much useless as far as anybody else could tell. Whenever I tried to explain that to Grandma, though, she'd just stare out across the wild flower field and over toward Cold River Mountains. She spent a lot of time that summer staring at those mountains with this far-away glaze in her eyes, as if she was looking at something no one else could see.

Turns out that's exactly what she was doing, but I didn't know that just yet.

Nobody in Owl Creek could understand why Grandma never went to visit the cemetery where her husband, son, and daughter-in-law were lined up waiting for her, but I knew why. Grandma hated the very idea of being pumped full of chemicals and who knows what-all and stuck in the ground in some lead-lined casket made to last through the apocalypse.

"It's unnatural, I tell you," she'd tell me. "Used to be a spirit got to leave this world free and clean, and the body went back to the earth. What do I want my body hangin' around after I'm done with it? Nope, I don't want my body sticking around here no longer than it has to."

I secretly thought Grandma's stubbornness about getting buried had more to do with the outrageous prices over at Abbott's Funeral Home than about setting her spirit free, but you try arguing with Grandma sometime and see how far you get.

It's a rotten thing to admit, but the road kill was keeping me too busy to fuss much about Grandma and her plans for the afterlife. I'd heard it around Owl Creek that there might be a bonus for the most road kill recorded before September. I was thinking maybe the bonus would be to keep that phone instead of having to turn it back to the government, and by then I really wanted that phone bad.

Someday you won't believe you ever put a lousy old phone in front of your own dying Grandma, but try telling that to an eighteen-year-old. Or maybe a part of me just didn't believe that there was anything fierce enough to come along and take Grandma from me, even though that summer I'd been learning a few up close and personal things about how death works.

Squatted down by the side of the road taking notes about some flattened raccoon or deer with its guts hanging out, I saw all the mysteries of decomposition firsthand. Turns out there are five stages, though most people probably don't know it: fresh, bloat, active, advanced decay, and dry remains. I knew Owl Creek County like the back of my hand, so I'd usually get to them in the fresh or bloat stage. That's when the blowflies and beetles would start arriving. Sometimes the gases would build up so much that a carcass would take to wheezing and gasping through its nose or mouth just like it was trying to whisper something to me from beyond the grave. You can bet that freaked me right out at first, but eventually I got used to it. It helped to pretend I was one of the forensics doctors on the crime shows me and Grandma always watched, even though the victim was a splattered opossum and I pretty much already knew some pick-up truck or speeding Chevy was the killer.

Even the maggots that would eventually show up like a pot of soggy rice thrown out the back porch door didn't bother me too much after a while. In fact, everything was going along just fine until Grandma decided that she wanted to come along with me on a hunt.

"Give me somethin' to do," she said as she followed me out of the house one otherwise fine August morning.

I knew she had to have something better to do than get her kidneys jogged around by the ancient shocks in Uncle Johnny's hatchback or else suffocate to death on account of the busted air-conditioner. But I've already told you about trying to argue with Grandma.

The first thing we came across was a deer that had been cut clean down the middle. One half of it was by the side of the road and the other half was a quarter mile away at the edge of one of those new housing developments that seem to just pop up one day when no one's looking.

"Crows and coyotes will soon come for this," Grandma said. She hitched up her skirt and leaned down like she was surveying the buffet counter at the Stop N' Eat.

"Not quick enough for the folks living here," I said, nodding toward the development. "Already stinks to high heaven in this heat."

"Folks have forgotten how to tolerate the smell of death is all," Grandma said. "Seems to me more and more folks is forgettin' to tolerate death altogether. All these bodies pumped full of chemicals and who knows what-all, refusin' to leave when their time's up."

I'd been afraid that road kill spotting would bring Grandma back to that point of contention, and I for one didn't want to talk about it anymore. But once Grandma got started on a thing, there wasn't no way I ever knew of to get her off it.

"Think about it, Levon," she said. "All those bodies lyin' around so that eventually the whole earth is covered in nothin' but bodies as far as the eye can see, one layered right on top of the other."

"It don't work that way, Grandma."

She gave me the sideways eye and snorted through her nose. "I'll tell you what don't work—turnin' a body inside out and stashin' it away like a jar of preserves is what don't work. Me, I don't want my body—"

"To stick around here no longer than it has to," I finished for her. "I know, 'cause you've told me a thousand times. C'mon, Grams, let's go." I took her by the arm and led her back to the car. Before she got in she turned back to look at the deer and that far away glaze came into her eyes.

"If the county don't come for it first, a deer like this can feed dozens of scavengers," she said. "Then once they get through with it, thousands more beetles and worms and flies will get their turn, right on down to the plants and the grass we're standin' on. Take a good look at how it works, Levon. Lots of livin' things depend on the death of another."

I had a dream that night where all kinds of images got mixed up and thrown together all crazy like they do sometimes in dreams: the torn-apart deer was there, then Momma hooked up to those machines in the hospital, too weak and out of her mind with pain in the end to even know where she was. I saw Papa go off to the lake one day and never come back, and Grandpa wasting away before his own eyes till there was nothing left to waste. And then I saw all three of them down in Shady View Cemetery, only they weren't lying side by side in their graves like they were supposed to be. Instead they were above the ground piled one on top of the other like stacks of hot cakes. I looked around and saw that everybody else in Shady View was the same way. Nobody was rotted away or anything, they were all just lying there one on top of the other like they were still alive, only they weren't. They were dead all right, only it was like they'd forgotten how to be dead and nobody had seen fit to come along and remind them.

The next day I forgot all about the dream, but I couldn't forget about Grandma's cough. And not even Grandma was stubborn enough to refuse to go to the doctor's once the blood started coming up. By then it was too late to do much about the tumors in her lungs, but she figured she was so old there wouldn't have been much they could do about them anyhow.

"There are certain things we can try to give you three, maybe four more months," the doctor said. "The human body is a funny thing. You never know what it's capable of."

"I know what this one's capable of," Grandma told him. "And what it *ain't* capable of just the same."

Ever since then Grandma had taken to staring out at the Cold River Mountains more than ever.

"You'll get the house and a little savings I been puttin' away," she told me one night when the air had just turned chill with the promise of autumn. The road kill program had shut down over a month ago and I hadn't ended up winning the bonus. It had turned out to be an all-expense paid weekend trip to Charleston, but by then I didn't care much about that phone anyway. I guess I was starting down the road to not being a kid anymore, even though I never would have guessed it then.

"Your uncles and aunts will help out until you get on your feet," she said. "Time you start gettin' out in the world anyway, Levon."

It wasn't the money I was worried about though. Back in August the doctors gave Grandma a month at best, and here it was almost October and she still wouldn't even consider going down to Abbott's Funeral Home.

"Law says you got to be buried," I reminded her about every day.

"But the law don't say how," she reminded me back.

The first frost had come in the night before, and for some reason I woke up early that morning or else I would have missed her altogether. It was still dark out, and something made me go down to the kitchen and look out the window across the wildflower field. I'd be lying if I said I was surprised to see Grandma wrapped up in her old red pea coat trekking toward Cold River Mountains.

That didn't stop me from racing out the door after her, though, or calling out to her so loud that a flock of blackbirds burst out of the trees like a scatter of buckshot.

"Grandma!"

She turned around and looked at me like she wasn't quite sure who I was, but she let me catch up to her just the same. Not like she could have outrun me, but for some reason I thought she might disappear into the mist before I could reach her.

"You never were one to miss a trick, Levon," she said. She put her wrinkled old hands on both my cheeks and looked into my face good and hard. "You may not be a healer like your mama was, but you got your own kind of touch just the same. You just got to figure out how best to use it."

She let go of my face and then turned around and started back across the field.

"Going to be cold up in them mountains, Grams," I said. My voice was shaking and I had to blink hard to keep my eyes dry.

"Aw, the mountains will keep me too busy to get cold, son. You've seen for yourself how much work there is for a body to do." Then she got that wicked tinkle in her eyes that she used to get with Grandpa when she'd had a few too many glasses of hard cider. "Say, you're not going to make a record of me and send it to the government, are you?"

I stood there with my mouth hanging open until Grandma burst out laughing, and then I burst out laughing, too.

"No, Grams," I told her. "Ain't nobody but them mountains gonna know where you been."

"But you'll always know where I *am*, Levon," she said, pointing across the field to our old house. "Just look out that window there or feel the breeze comin' off the mountains, and you'll always know where to find me."

I watched her disappear across the field until all I could see was a little red dot, and then even that vanished in the mist. I ran all the way back home and sat there in the kitchen not knowing what to do next. The sun was coming up before I figured out that there really wasn't nothing I *could* do next. Eventually I'd have to tell someone Grandma went missing. They'd form a search party and hunt around for her, but probably not for too long.

"Lots of them old-timers just disappear up into the mountains 'round here," I imagined Sheriff McBain would say. "Not a bad way to go, if you think about it."

I was scared of going to bed that night because of what I might dream. I didn't think I was ready to see Grandma again just yet. But it turns out I fell straight asleep and didn't wake up until the sun was high up in the sky.

The television was set to the weather channel and I sat in front of it for company while I ate my cereal. The house was a different place without Grandma in it, but I figured I'd have to start getting used to that.

"Looks like summer is set to make one last visit to southern West Virginia, folks," the weatherman said. "It's eighty-six degrees already here in Charleston and we could set a record if the temperatures keep climbing."

I turned off the T.V. and went to the kitchen window. The wildflowers were shimmering in the afternoon heat and the mist had burned off the mountains.

"Should have known you'd bully the weather into helpin' you get your way, Grams," I said, watching the red line climb on the thermometer stuck on the outside window sill. "Looks like you won't have to stick around here hardly no time at all."

Grief Assassins

The pillowcase finally stopped smelling of him.

For the past seven months the first thing she'd done in the morning was smell that pillowcase. Even when Romero stood on her chest rubbing his head against her and yowling for breakfast, Marquisha made him wait while she buried her face in the sweaty-musky hair oil smell that never failed to make her cry.

She had cherished those tears as much as she cherished the smell, and now it was gone.

Some of his shirts still had traces of his scent, but nothing close to the raw, intimate smell of the pillowcase. She'd picked up some lingering hints of him on an old blanket in the attic, but it couldn't compete with the pungent contributions from the dogs who'd shared it with him for so many years.

The first one had been named Lundi, a big old slobbering clown of a dog that loved Ron so much that if he was out of sight for even a minute, she'd turn in circles and whimper until he reappeared. Ron had eventually given in to her constant presence, even letting her into the bathroom with him.

"How wrong is that with a dog sitting there staring you down when you're trying to do your morning business?" he said.

Marquisha would just laugh and say, "Hey, baby, that's what you get for being such a ladies' man."

When Lundi died, Ron had been so devastated it had taken him a long time to get interested in the idea of another dog.

"If you lost your best human friend, you wouldn't just go replacing her right off the bat like that, would you?" he'd scolded Marquisha when she'd first brought it up. It had taken another two years before Ron had finally fell in love with a little scrapper down at the shelter, but his favorite picture of Lundi had stayed in the prize place on the living room bookshelf just the same.

Both those dogs were gone now, and so was Ron. Nine months ago, an aneurism had torn through his otherwise healthy forty-seven-year old brain while he was out shooting hoops with the old gang from high school. In the split-second it took to hear, "I'm sorry, he's gone," Marquisha learned that a person doesn't just die and take nothing along for the ride—an entire world dies with him. The one Ron took with him had been Marquisha's world, too.

"Just give yourself some time, honey," her mother told her. "When your father died I didn't know how I'd get through one minute without him let alone the rest of my life. And look at me now! Sure I still miss him, every day. But life goes on."

Life goes on. Give it time. Keep busy. Get out more.

But Marquisha knew that giving it time wasn't going to change things. With every day that went by, she grew more and more certain that no amount of time existed that would ever make her want to replace not just her best friend and husband, but her entire world. When

Ron died, the person she was to him died, too. And that's the only person she had ever wanted to be.

Marquisha pulled the case off the pillow and tossed it into the hamper. No sense refusing to wash it anymore. And with the last traces of Ron slowly disappearing from her life, there was no sense keeping up the charade any longer, either.

The plain metal box was tucked away on the top shelf of the closet like a particularly ominous-looking Christmas present. Marquisha supposed that in a morbid sort of way, it was.

Unwrapping it was as easy as snapping open the lid, and this gift came fully loaded and ready to go. Marquisha clicked off the safety and tested the feel of it in her hand. Even though she'd done it many times before, she was always surprised at the pistol's reassuring weight, the satisfying way her fingers wrapped around the handle.

She felt Romero curling around her legs. She couldn't look into those imploring amber eyes right now, but she did lean down and scratch behind his ear.

"Don't you worry, Romero," she whispered. "You'll be taken care of. I've made sure of that much. Besides, you always did like your grandma's house way out in the country."

Marquisha caught sight of herself in the mirror on the opposite side of the room. The otherwise ordinary woman standing there with a .22 automatic pistol in her hand didn't look like she was about ready to put it against the side of her head and pull the trigger. But looks could

He still remembered losing his first one. Tanu had told him, "Every now and then a human being just doesn't want to stay any longer. We do what we can, but in the end we must respect that choice."

And Alik did respect it. But he also knew that sometimes humans made that choice a little too quickly, a little too rashly. That's when the temptations came over him.

It was technically impossible to cross zones and enter the human world, but a rogue agent had taught him the trick.

"The higher ups don't want you to know it," she'd told him. "But as long as humans are not in a conscious state of mind—if they're asleep, say, or passed out—you can walk around their world just as big as you please."

It was strictly forbidden to directly interfere with humans, of course. Alik eventually heard that the rogue agent had been decommissioned and sent to a corrective unit for reconditioning.

He had resisted for a long time, but the urge to touch a human, to feel the warmth and life behind their skin even once, had ultimately proven too strong. He knew what the consequences would be if he ever got caught, so he reserved the experience for rare occasions.

Marquisha had been one of those occasions.

He had come to her one night not long after getting the assignment. Her skin had been impossible to resist, as smooth and dark as the satin sheets she wound so fitfully around her at night. Alik had pressed his hand against her cheek and she had softly moaned the name of her beloved. Her bottomless well of pain had almost swallowed him whole. And yet it wasn't an entirely empty well, either. There was still love and passion and life in there along with all that pain. It just hadn't found its way to the surface yet.

Now she was standing there with her hand wrapped around a pistol that would end any chance that it ever would. If he was going to act, it would have to be now. He was, after all, a Grief Assassin. That's the job he had been sent to do, and this time he was going to do it right.

He concentrated on her thoughts again and this time he caught hold of it. The grief hit him with the cold-shock jolt that always knocked him back a little, even after so many times. Only this time, things were going to be different. This time he wasn't going to kill off only the biggest, meanest griefs and just go home. This time he was going to kill off every single last sneaky one of them.

When it was finished, Marquisha was lying unconscious on the floor. Most humans didn't make it through the process without passing out. When she awoke, she wouldn't remember anything about what had happened.

Once a case was finished, agents were not permitted to see the human again. This would be his only chance to slip the barrier and touch her one last time.

His sudden appearance caused the black and white cat to blast out of the room like a police cruiser on a chase. Alik knelt on the floor beside her and touched that warm, wondrous skin. Maybe he was just imagining it, but he thought she looked more peaceful already.

ago and found the poor thing almost starved to death? How in the world could Marquisha have just 'forgotten' to feed it like she said?"

As if understanding that he was the subject of the present discussion, the black and white cat wound through the kitchen and jumped up on Lorraine's ample lap.

"Don't get me wrong, I don't mind having the little fellow here one bit," she said. "But I just can't for the life of me understand why I had to take the poor thing away from Marquisha in the first place and, worse yet, why it seemed like she could have cared one bit less when I did."

Jackie sipped her tea and tried to come up with an answer for what she had to admit was some strange behavior coming from her niece lately. "It's like you always say," she finally told her sister. "People have all kinds of different ways of dealing with their grief."

The man was lying face down in the entryway of the store. It looked like he had blood coming out of one side of his nose. Marquisha looked around for help, but it was still too early for the morning rush.

She had been coming to work early for over a week now in order to get an exact fix on when her boss would be in the office alone. She had figured out the perfect window of time after the janitor left and before the early birds started trickling in. Luckily her boss was a woman of very regular habits, one of which was to always be the first one in the office. Habits like that had earned her the respect of the people who worked for her, including Marquisha—which is why her plan to show up at the office tomorrow morning and put a bullet into her boss's brain was nothing personal.

The man on the ground rolled over and moaned. Marquisha was ready to dial 911 when she noticed that her phone battery was almost dead. She had a lot of important calls to make this morning that definitely needed to be private. It took her phone a couple of hours to recharge and she just didn't have that kind of time to lose.

Marquisha tucked her phone back into her bag and kept walking without giving the injured man another thought.

"You did *what?*" Tanu asked for at least the fourth time in a row. "You did *what?*" he repeated, adding a fifth.

Alik had already provided a more-or-less accurate answer to the question, so he waited in silence as Tanu fumed.

"And you waited *this long* to tell me! Do you have any *idea* how bad this is?"

This time he seemed to want an answer. "I didn't think it would get this bad," Alik said.

Which was true, actually. Of course he'd had to go back and check on her. He'd broken so many rules by then, what did one more matter?

Straight away he'd noticed that her eyes had changed. The soft, inquisitive kindness had been replaced with something harder. But Alik thought that might be a good thing. A little hardness was necessary in

"You still talk to Ursa over in the Memory Keepers unit?" Alik asked.

"As if I could ever stop talking to Ursa."

"Does she still owe you a favor for helping her out of that jam with the Pleasure Accelerators?"

"Yeah, she still owes me. I'm guessing she won't after this, though."

"Look, I'll owe you the mother of all favors if you cash yours in with her on this one. I've got all the memories I need right up here," Alik said, tapping his head. He'd never reported to Mind Clearance after Marquisha's case ended, and now he was damn glad for his negligence. "I just need Ursa to work a little transferal magic for me, and a guy I know over in Sensory Regulation can do the rest."

The alarm went off early and Marquisha rolled over to shut it off. Today was the day she was going to eliminate the woman who wanted to eliminate her from her job. She didn't look forward to it, but like so many other things in life, it had to be done.

She was almost out of bed when something hit her that was so strange, yet so familiar, that at first she couldn't quite place it. Only when she looked down at the pillow next to hers, encased in the crumpled pillowcase she'd almost forgotten, did she remember.

It smelled like him. The pillowcase had the sweaty-musky hair oil smell that belonged to only one person—Ron, her beloved husband.

She couldn't remember the last time she'd thought about him or his smell.

Marquisha leaned out of bed because suddenly she felt as if she might throw up, as if something rotten had been fermenting inside of her for months and had to come out. She choked back the taste of bile in her throat and buried her face in the pillow.

She had almost forgotten what that smell was like. She sat up and looked around her bedroom as if waking from a long sleep. Marquisha realized that she'd almost forgotten a lot.

The pillowcase was wet against her cheek, and it took Marquisha a moment to realize it was from her tears. She hadn't cried in a long time, and it felt good now. It felt like a release and an embrace all at the same time. Marquisha held onto the pillow and let the flood come.

When he was sure that she'd finally fallen back to sleep, Alik allowed himself one last time. Tanu was a good friend, and he would keep Alik's secret—this time. But Tanu was also a good agent, and Alik knew that he wouldn't get any more mistakes like this one. He wanted to remain a Grief Assassin, not in spite of what had happened with Marquisha, but because of it.

He now finally understood grief enough to work with it instead of against it. Maybe that's what Tanu had been trying to teach him all along.

Alik leaned down and touched Marquisha's cheek for what he knew would be the last time. He already had an appointment with Mind

Clearance first thing in the morning, and he was going to keep it this time. By tomorrow afternoon, he wouldn't even remember her name.

He had already made up his mind to leave the pillow case here this time. It would eventually lose the beloved's smell again, and maybe Marquisha would end up in the exact same place she'd been when he'd stepped too far into her fate. But maybe she wouldn't. Either way, she loved again and she hurt again—she *felt* again. Alik had learned that was what really counted, no matter how it turned out.

He looked at her one last time before crossing back to his own zone. "You're going to be just fine," he whispered, and this time he knew his words would reach her.

Age Will Be Responsible

When the eight-inch water bug ran across the toe of the real estate lady's high-heeled shoe, Jodie thought for sure she was going to turn around and run straight up the stairs without so much as a backward glance. When that didn't happen, he pointed to the rows of glue traps lining the basement walls.

"See all them with their legs in the air? That one will get caught just the same, give it time," he told her.

The real estate lady gave him a look that said she considered him as nasty as the water bugs, but Jodie just smiled. Even with the double wages the development company was paying, he knew that no one was exactly lining up to take this job.

"So how long do you think it's going to take to clear these out? The company wants the building resold in, let's see..." She stabbed a few times at that little pad she was always staring at and then finished without looking up. "Six months, max."

Jodie nudged the edge of a giant steamer trunk with the tip of his work boot. Like all of the others, it was caked with grime and dust, the peeling shipping stickers on the side a faded reminder of the lost pleasures of "The Cunard White Star" and "Hotel Continental Paris."

"Bet this one hasn't been moved in forty years or more," Jodie said. "Can you imagine what would come running out from under there?"

"I'd rather not," the real estate lady said.

The air in the basement was dank and unsanitary. Jodie knew she was itching to get out of there—which made it even more fun to keep her there a little bit longer.

"And you say I can keep anything I turn up down here?" he asked.

"Like I've told you already, we sent letters to everyone we could find. But most of this junk belongs to people who haven't been alive for decades, so whatever hasn't been claimed by now has to go. And the sooner the better, because it's important—"

But whatever was important was cut short by an ear-piercing scream. The real estate lady's shoe had introduced itself to another of the residents. This time it was a desiccated rat carcass. That *was* enough to send her running for the stairs, and Jodie watched her slender legs disappear up the rickety steps.

Alone with the water bugs and sprouting mold spores, Jodie fingered a torn green tag attached to an imitation leather suitcase with bulging seams longing to spill its secrets. The color of the tags showed the last time they had been handled—red meant the nineties, green the eighties, orange the seventies, and so on. The graying white tags went all the way back to the fifties or even, in some cases, the forties.

"Those must have been the days," Jodie muttered to the gloom. "Porters in starched shirts and bow-ties fetching trunks for movie stars and big shots. Yep, those were the Hollywood golden days all right. Been a steady downhill trip ever since."

Golden days or not, the trunks and suitcases stored down here had been forgotten about for a reason—most of them were empty, and the rest contained nothing but old, useless junk. Jodie had been through about half of them already, and so far all he'd turned up was a tangled mass of Marine Corps ammo belts in a trunk with the name "T.R. Moukad" stenciled on the side; a pile of cancelled checks from the year 1952 in a tattered paisley carpet bag; and an eggshell blue hard-side with a broken lock and a collection of Village People records inside.

If any hidden treasures were buried down here, Jodie hadn't found them yet.

He had hold of the rusted chain that worked the room's only light bulb when the small brown trunk caught his eye. It was just as grimy as the rest of them, but something about it seemed different— important somehow, as if it had been down here all of these years just waiting to be found. The tag was gray-white and half-disintegrated.

Jodie tried the latch, but it was locked. He took out his pocketknife and pried at it for a while, but it wouldn't budge.

"Flimsy little lock's no bigger than a matchbook, yet look how it holds! They don't make 'em like that anymore, I'll tell you that."

He called up the stairs to see if the real estate lady was still around, but no one answered back. Was he only allowed to take stuff *from* the bags, or could he take the whole thing?

"What the hell, they're all gonna be dumped anyway."

The trunk was surprisingly light in his hand—so much for hidden bars of gold or bottles of rare whiskey. He switched off the bulb and climbed the warped stairs that protested beneath his bulk. Only when the light from the first floor sent a shaft through the open stairway door did he see the hand-written sign. He'd been down in the basement dozens of times but somehow he'd never noticed it before.

At one time it had read, "The management will not be responsible for articles stored in basement," but dust, grime, and disintegration had obscured some of the letters.

"Ha-ha, would ya look at that!" Jodie said. He had the lifelong loner's habit of talking to himself out loud and sometimes even answering. "Way it reads now looks like 'Age will be responsible for articles stored in basement.' Age will be responsible! Now that's the truth if ever I heard it!"

Jodie had meant to break the lock off and see what was inside right away, but the cats kept crying for their dinner and more notices from the real estate company were in the mail, so by the time he settled in front of the TV with his own warmed up plastic tray, he'd forgotten all about the little suitcase. He had just drifted off to an old comedy when he heard it—calliope music, like the kind they played at a circus—but no, that wasn't quite it. The same refrain seemed to repeat itself over and over again, and he felt the hair stand up on the back of his neck. He seemed to recall that same kind of music from a summer night a long time ago, but the memory skittered away from him like a spider escaping through a crack in the wall.

Where was that damn music coming from, anyway?

He stood up and went to the door. "Lousy musicians need to cut that out this late at night."

Only Jodie knew that there weren't any musicians left in the building. In fact, there wasn't *anybody* left in the building except for him. He wasn't even sure if the company taking over from the last one was going to renovate it or just raze the whole thing to the ground. If that happened, he'd be out of luck and how. With rent control, social security, and the little extra he got doing odd jobs around the place, he had enough left over at the end of the month to get by. But not by much, and ever since Hollywood had decided to reinvent itself with fancy shopping centers and luxury apartment buildings, rent had gone through the roof all over town. Now he'd be lucky if he could even afford some downtown hole-in-the-wall.

He opened the door and gazed both ways down the hallway. The dirty orange carpet with the zigzag pattern gave him vertigo just like it had been doing for the past twenty years. But the hallway was empty, and the music seemed to have stopped.

"Too many damn crazy musicians in Hollywood, that's the trouble."

The last of his mashed potatoes and steak pie had gone cold, and he put the plastic tray on the floor for the cats to finish off. Maybe that trunk would have something in it that would solve his problems, even if it wasn't bars of gold. Maybe stacks of lost gangster money or some old movie star secrets that would fetch something from a collector. He went and got a pair of pliers, and by the time he had the lock pried off he was already thinking about that new high-rise on the corner of Vine, the one with the cabana bar on the roof.

"Ah, damn it to hell anyway..."

All that was inside was a tissue-thin wedding dress carefully folded inside yellowing sheets of newspaper. He took the dress out of the paper, studied its intricate patterns of silk and lace, and then carefully laid it back in the trunk.

"Damn thing looks like it'll to turn to dust if you so much as looked at it too long."

He smoothed the newspaper out on the floor and cheered up a little when he saw the date: Wednesday, May 9, 1945. It might be worth something to a World War II collector or history buff.

The paper was called *The Star*. It came from the Island of Guernsey, and only one headline blared across the top: "RELIEVED! British Troops Arrive in Guernsey."

Jodie remembered a documentary he'd seen on TV about the Channel Islands. "Only part of Britain to be occupied by German forces," he reminded himself. Jodie knew a lot about military history even though he himself had never served on account of his weak feet.

He scanned the rest of the paper. It mostly had articles about how food and tobacco provisions were on the way and pictures of crowds cheering in the streets with the British flag being raised and all that happy patriotic horseshit. One headline in particular caught his eye and inspired a chuckle as greasy and unsavory as the last of his dinner congealing in its plastic tray: "Guernsey Men Return to Island with the Liberators."

"And I wonder what the Guernsey women were getting up to while they were gone," Jodie snorted.

He lumbered up from the floor and fingered the wedding gown nestled quietly in the case. The lace and gauze were so fragile that the dress seemed ready to crumble in his hands.

"Looks like this young bride's man either didn't return home with the liberators or didn't want her anymore once he did."

He folded up the brittle newspaper and tossed it back in the trunk on top of the dress. Tomorrow he'd take the whole thing to a collector he knew on Fairfax and accept whatever offer he could get.

The calliope music was getting louder and louder, faster and faster, and the big grinning faces spun round and round until Jodie thought his head would spin right off with them. Then all of a sudden the music stopped. The woman came out of nowhere, silent and dressed in a white gown... a wedding gown. She was holding a bouquet of red flowers just below her waistline. A curtain of dark hair prevented Jodie from seeing her face, but he thought she was smiling—smiling at *him*.

He groaned as a long dormant desire—hell, long *dead* as far as he'd figured—flared back to life. The woman reached toward him. Jodie reached back, but as their hands connected he saw that where the red bouquet of flowers had been was now an ugly red stain between her legs, seeping outward across the white of the dress like an angry crimson sunrise.

The calliope music started again and Jodie tried to scream, but all of a sudden his throat closed up as if cold, slender hands were squeezing it tight...

He bolted up in bed as his strangled cry sent the cats flying in all directions. "Dammit, anyway! I've got to lay off of that whiskey before bed."

He'd overslept and had to work harder than he liked in order to finish his chores. He fixed the broken gate at the back and cleaned out the front garden boxes even though nothing had grown in them for a decade at least. But he didn't go back down to the basement. All day the terrible dream about the woman in white stayed with him. And that maddening calliope music hummed in his ears like a gnat that keeps coming back no matter how many times you swat it away.

But more than anything else, the crimson stain between the woman's legs contaminated his every thought.

By the time Jodie got back to his apartment and fed the cats and himself, he was too exhausted to even think about going all the way to Fairfax. The trunk was still on the hall table where he'd left it. He went over and squinted at the faded gray tag. He could just make out the owner's name if he filled in some letters here and there.

"Eileen Livingston or Livingstone or some damn thing like that. A lady-like name all right, but it sure as hell isn't lady-like to scare a harmless old man in the middle of the night."

He poured his nightly whiskey and had a good laugh at himself before going to bed.

"Must finally be getting soft in the head," he told the cats as he drifted into sleep.

In his dream that night Jodie was dressed in a crisp uniform with tall black boots. He felt more confident and powerful than he ever had in his real life. The woman with the curtain of dark hair was in a crowded dance hall this time, but she wasn't wearing white. Instead she was in a fancy striped number with shiny black shoes; it looked like she'd spent a lot of time getting ready. He knew that the local girls weren't supposed to dance with the Germans, but girls need to have some fun now and then. They need to dance and laugh and feel special, even during wartime—maybe especially during wartime. Jodie caught the dark-haired woman's eye and they danced round and round to the music—that same calliope tune again. She was smiling, wide and radiant, and then somehow they were out by the sea. The gritty, damp sand was rough beneath their skin; the cold, salty water misted their faces and hair.

The woman was beside him on the sand, but she wasn't smiling anymore. She was telling him to stop, please stop, but the desire rose up in him, an animal thing, and he couldn't stop now—wouldn't stop.

The crashing waves must have drowned everything else out, because he never heard the old man approaching. By the time he registered the startled cry and outraged expression it was too late. Of course they'd both been recognized; in a town like Guernsey, everyone knew everybody else—and everything *about* everybody else. Tomorrow the entire island would know about the pretty-dark haired girl and the German officer.

He hadn't even stepped in the door of headquarters the next morning before his commanding officer summed him.

"There has been some disturbing talk among the people about a local girl caught in a, shall we say, compromising position with one of our officers last night."

The sweat crept across his forehead like a sticky confession, but he remained silent as long as he could.

"You know, of course, how important it is to maintain good relations with the natives of this island, *Ober-Leutenant*? How crucial it is to show the British what civilized occupiers we will be once we take the rest of their country, yes?"

"Yes, *Hauptsturmführer*!"

"And so, of course, any crime against the native population will be punished by the severest measure of our laws. That is as it should be, don't you agree?"

"Yes, Hauptsturmführer!"

His commander stood up and came within inches of his face. Jodie—or whoever the hell he was in the dream—could smell the coffee he'd had for breakfast still on his breath.

"And do you know what the punishment is for, say, raping a civilian woman, Ober-Leutenant?"

"Yes, sir! Military execution, sir."

"That is correct! Death by firing squad. This sends quite a clear message to our British hosts that such savagery will not be tolerated."

The commander sat back down and Jodie had to force his legs to keep holding him upright.

"And do you think we will we be getting any reports of such misbehavior, Ober-Leutenant?"

"No, sir!"

"Then you are dismissed, Ober-Leutenant. And for both of our sakes, I hope you are correct."

He had never asked the dark-haired woman to lie for him. In fact, he'd never even spoken to her again. At first, he'd waited every day for the arrest order to come and had almost reconciled himself to his fate. But then he'd seen the dark-haired woman in the market. The other women turned her away from their stalls. The men spit at her and called out "Jerry-bag" and "German's whore" when she walked by. He knew then that he was safe—he knew that for some reason he would never begin to understand, the woman had destroyed her own reputation for the sake of preserving his life.

Less than a month later he received his orders for the Russian front. He never went back to the British Isles; the dark-haired woman was eventually forgotten. But little towns like Guernsey have very long memories. Long after the dark-haired woman's fiancé returned home from the war and broke off the engagement, long after she boarded the ship that would take her to the United States and a new life, Eileen Livingstone would be known as Guernsey's German whore.

Jodie woke up in the middle of the night covered in sweat. He stumbled out of bed and poured himself a shot of whiskey with trembling hands, and then another. What in the hell was the matter with him? Why was he dreaming about being a Nazi, about some long-dead woman whose name he'd read on a luggage tag? Hell, he'd never even been out of California let alone overseas!

He looked around for his cats but none were in sight. "Where are you rotten felines hiding?"

The trunk was on the hall table, silent and inscrutable. Jodie glanced at it and then did a double-take. The lid was wide open, but he was *sure* he'd left it closed.

His feet made the decision to walk toward it without the consent of his nerves. All of a sudden that damn calliope music began to play, like at a circus or a carnival…

Jodie stumbled backward and cried out in the darkened hallway. He suddenly remembered exactly when and where he'd last heard that music. It had been a long time ago, a summer night underneath the pier at Santa Monica. The gritty, damp sand was rough beneath their skin; the cold, salty water misted their faces and hair. The woman—not the one with the curtain of dark hair, not Eileen Livingston or Livingstone or whatever the hell her name was—but *his* dancing partner, the one with wheat-colored curls and a sweet, crooked smile. But just like Eileen

Livingstone and her Nazi, she had told him to stop, please stop. But the desire had risen up in him, an animal thing, and he couldn't stop now—wouldn't stop.

Only Jodie hadn't been as lucky as the German. The girl with the wheat-colored curls hadn't been willing to risk her reputation for his sake, even if it wasn't a matter of life and death. In fact, on that freezing sand with the calliope music swirling through the air, she had told Jodie that she was going to first tell her father and then the police. He couldn't let that happen, could he?

She should have kept her mouth shut, like that Guernsey girl. But just like a good lock on a sturdy piece of luggage, they didn't make women like that anymore.

He'd had to make sure this one stayed silent. It had been easy enough to choke the words right out of her with just a little pressure to the sides of her neck.

What was one more missing girl in a city full of missing girls—hell, a whole *world* full of missing girls just like Eileen Livingstone with nothing left behind but a forgotten suitcase in a cobweb covered basement.

Jodie heard a low, animal growling. He wasn't sure if it had come from him or the missing cats. The paper-thin white dress glowed in the dim hallway like a patch of sickly moonlight. His hands were even more defiant against his nerves than his feet had been, because even though it was the last thing in the world he wanted to touch, he reached into the suitcase and picked up the dress. He held it by the shoulders and shook loose the careful folds of time.

The dress fell full-length to the floor. Jodie saw a red stain just below the waist, spreading outward like an angry crimson sunrise.

He tried to scream, but no sound came out. All of a sudden his throat closed up as if cold, slender hands were squeezing it tight, choking the scream right out of him with just a little pressure to the sides of his neck...

"They say he was in here for like, two days or something before anyone finally found him."

The well-dressed real estate lady in the high-heeled shoes gave her young assistant a disgusted look and then sighed. "Just what this building needs—one more mess to clean up. Time to tell management to stop being cheap and hire a real cleaning crew."

They were on their way out of the apartment when the trunk on the hall table caught the woman's eye. She opened the lid. All that was inside was a tissue-thin wedding dress carefully folded inside yellowing sheets of newspaper.

"I wonder why that old guy wanted something like this?" she asked.

"Must have thought it was worth something," her assistant said.

"Maybe he was being sentimental. Although he didn't strike me as the sentimental type. Might as well leave it for the clean-up crew."

The key was already in the front door lock when the woman hesitated. She went back to the trunk and unfolded the wedding dress so that it fell full-length to the floor. It was in excellent condition for its age—crisp and white without a single spot or blemish. She was friendly with a woman who owned a little shop on Ivar that specialized in vintage clothing. Maybe it was something that would interest her.

She folded the dress back into the trunk, closed the lid, and tucked it under her arm. After all, she told herself, one man's junk is another man's treasure, and there might be someone out there just waiting to rediscover this little piece of history.

Released

Impossible to tell how many days. Maybe enough to pile into months, or even years, for all you know of time. Time was one of the first things to go.

Your body, though, went even quicker than time. A trickle of sweat that might have been tears prompts you to wipe your eyes. Only then do you realize that you can't wipe your eyes or anything else. You are as bound to this bed as an object embedded in cement.

The word "trapped" has an entirely new meaning to you now.

Trapped: (adjective) caught in a trap. Synonyms for trapped: deceived; captured; ambushed; cornered; tangled; at bay.

Trap: (noun) 1: a device for taking game or other animals; *especially*: one that holds by springing shut suddenly 2: something by which one is caught or stopped unawares; *also*: a position or situation from which it is difficult or impossible to escape.

A fly tickling across your nose is a nuisance to be quickly flicked away. A fly tickling across your nose that cannot be flicked away quickly becomes much more than a nuisance. A hand that flicks the fly away is a welcome relief even when you have no idea to whom the hand belongs.

An unknown hand belonging to an unknown body can either help or harm. Or both.

You are surrounded by blackness. Your eyes have forgotten how to see.

You're given food, possibly by the same hand that flicks the fly. You assume that you eat it even though you no longer recognize the taste or texture. It has been too long for taste or texture.

There used to be voices. Sometimes you still hear them, faintly, but not as often as you used to. It has been too long for voices.

The important sound now is the clang of metal against metal, steel making contact with steel. The even more important sound is the whisper of footsteps outside the door. You used to follow the patterns of coming and going, but it has been too long for patterns.

The footsteps are connected to the metal and steel. Your existence is connected to the metal and steel.

You are fairly certain that you are still alive, though it has been too long to be certain what living means any more.

A memory: the smell of feet and rubber yoga mats; instructor's gray hair wound serpentine around colorful scarves. "Rise out of your skin and float freely. Your mind will rejoin your body when both feel safe with each other again."

Mind-body dissociation; detachment of physical self.

Question you would now like to ask: What if some minds and bodies never feel safe with each other again?

Skin is something that you still remember—sunlight on skin; the warmth of skin; the smell of his skin; goose bumps on skin; tingling skin. Tormented skin. If you knew that you would feel skin on skin even one more time, you might survive this starvation of it.

Do not notice the signs that tell you others have been in this room before you. Do not wonder how long they were trapped. Do not consider how they got out.

Fact: There is no way out.

Another memory: Russian professor, thick glasses. Lecture topic: touch depravation. "If a lack of tactile stimulation continues for a sufficient length of time, it may lead to serious developmental and emotional disturbances, such as stunted growth, personality disorders, and social regression. In severe cases, a child who is deprived of adequate physical handling and emotional stimulation may not survive infancy."

Question you would now like to ask: In severe cases, how long will an adult who is deprived of adequate physical handling and emotional stimulation *wish* to survive?

The last memory: a lonely road, a stormy night, a dead car engine, no phone service. Maybe a scene out of a horror movie, but no, you are inside the car, and you are no actor. At such moments it may be helpful to recall the rules:

"Lock the doors and windows and don't open up for anyone."

"Have a weapon within reach at all times, preferably something heavy enough to knock someone out with one quick blow to the head."

Most important rule of all: "Stay inside the car and wait until official help arrives."

A most important rule you chose to ignore, although you did take care to retrieve the tire iron from the trunk before standing on the side of the road waving your arms around in a universal sign of distress. The tire iron in your hand is a somewhat less universal sign that although you cannot fix a broken automobile, you are fully capable of knocking someone out with one quick blow to the head.

Or not.

When an automobile approaches on a deserted highway late at night, you can take some comfort in the fact that the automobile is a suburban family-of-four hatchback. However, if the only occupant inside of the reassuring automobile is male, you might have some cause for concern.

Helpful Hint: When in an uncertain situation with a potentially dangerous stranger, his facial expressions and body language may give some indication of his intentions.

Unhelpful Reality: In uncertain situations with a potentially dangerous stranger, faces are often no more than a blur. Especially when the uncertain situation takes place in the dark, as most uncertain situations tend to do.

Dark faces, dark highway, dark night.

Or at least what you used to think of as dark. Now you realize that you never really knew darkness at all. At least not the utter, absolute kind that swallows up safety and comfort and trust with one whale-jaw snap of black hole vastness.

Trapped.

If you had known about that kind of darkness, you never would have taken your chances against it.

Waking up somewhere that ends up being nowhere, in utter darkness, utterly alone. You haven't lived a perfect life, but you know this much: no hell could be as empty as this.

Resist the impulse to obsessively catalog what you could have done differently. Know that this is not your fault. Accept the unfairness of life. Permit yourself the hope that they have not forgotten about you. Stifle the urge to cry out for help.

Most Important Rule of All: Never, ever start thinking about what is going to happen to you next.

If the footsteps outside the door become more strident, it does not necessarily indicate a new purpose or design.

Certain sharp objects remind you of cat claws.

Fact: A cat will "play" with its prey in order to tire it out and reduce the risk of injury to itself. If the prey is lively, the cat could suffer a serious bite that might become infected and lead to death. Only when the prey is sufficiently tired and dazed is the cat able to make the kill.

You think about the relationship between cruelty and necessity. You wonder if you are sufficiently tired and dazed. You remind yourself of the Most Important Rule of All.

You think about anything other than what is going to happen to you next until you run out of things to think about.

Note to self: thinking about nothing is not as easy as it seems.

You cling to the memories as long as the memories allow: an ivy-covered house; sun-yellow walls; orange tea kettle; gray-velvet fur. Fields of drought-dry grass; cold water streams; shy, silent moons.

Eggshell-speckled eyes; dark mole on left shoulder blade; crooked pirate smile; long-fingered hands.

Memories like ghosts that haven't yet figured out a good way to die.

But even ghosts eventually die. Everything eventually dies.

Question: How long is eventually?

Fact: Just because you feel like you are dead doesn't mean that you are.

Another fact: Just because you wish that you were dead doesn't mean that you will be.

Refuse to consider things such as the disposal of your bodily waste and how you are being kept hygienically clean. Hands upon your body that your body no longer feels. Violations of your body that your body no longer registers.

Resign yourself to the fact that the hand that flicks away the flies now controls every aspect of your fate.

Observe the way that space moves around you now instead of you moving around it. Wonder how long a person can go without speaking before language is lost for good. Begin to understand why most prisoners choose physical punishment over solitary confinement. Contemplate how a person judges insanity with no other comparisons at hand.

Resist the idea that "someone will come and get me out of this place."

Remind yourself that miracles occur infrequently and arbitrarily. Remember that recent human history suggests they might not occur at all.

Keep believing in them anyway.

Impossible to tell how many days. Sleep has become your most important ally. Sleep is a triumph over the timelessness of time. In moments of extreme desperation, picture his face over and over until sleep arrives.

Sleep feels a little like what you think death should be.

Ignore the strange sounds outside the door that tell you something different is about to take place.

It is often possible to sense the presence of another person without direct proof that he or she is in the room. It is sometimes possible to feel an increase in activity without direct evidence of what is happening. It is occasionally possible to predict when an important decision is being made without direct involvement in what that decision will be.

It is usually impossible to believe that you have reached the end even though everything must end sometime.

When the hands are upon you more intensely than before, don't dwell upon the implications. When the arms seize you more fiercely than before, don't ponder the outcome.

Remind yourself that eventually all endings end.

Wonder if the liquid hitting your face comes from tears or sweat or something else. Calculate that the tears (or sweat or something else) are connected to the increased urgency of the hands and arms.

Rise out of your skin and float freely. Your mind will rejoin your body when both feel safe with each other again.

You recognize someone who resembles yourself lying on a hospital bed below where you are now floating. The room is no longer dark. The faces are no longer blurry, the voices no longer too faint to hear. One of the faces and voices belongs to him—

Him with the eggshell-speckled eyes, dark mole on left shoulder blade, crooked pirate smile, and long-fingered hands.

Clarify that the liquid hitting your face comes from tears, and the tears come from him.

Watch him hug the people in the room. Recognize the faces of the people.

Remember the last memory:

The reassuring hatchback on a dark road at night. The rain on the windshield, the sole male occupant of the car slowing too quickly, swerving too late. Notice someone who resembles yourself lying crumpled and broken by the side of the road, the tire iron flung into the weeds to be unearthed a decade later by two boys thrilled with their rusted discovery. Resist the urge to tell the frantic man crouched beside the broken body that there is no phone service here.

Watch the lights and listen to the sirens until the utter, absolute blackness swallows up safety and comfort and trust with one whale-jaw snap of black hole vastness.

Timeless. Comatose. Mind-body dissociation. Brain dead, body dead, not dead. Detachment of physical self.

Observe him with the eggshell-speckled eyes nod to a woman in a white uniform standing near a row of machines by your bedside. Watch the white uniform turning knobs, lowering switches. Resist the urge to reflect upon this development.

You are floating higher now, preparing for flight. The childhood dream of conquering air. Concentrate on keeping sight of your body. Once you lose sight of your body, you will no longer be able to return.

You are ready, but you wish to see him happy before you go. You want to thank him for not forgetting about you, for coming to get you out of this place. You want to tell him that you know the courage it takes, the scars it will leave.

Most of all you want him to understand.

Release: (transitive verb) 1: to set free from restraint, confinement, or servitude; *also*: to let go: dismiss 2: to relieve from something that confines, burdens, or oppresses 3: to give up in favor of another.

You wish to feel skin upon skin even one more time.

Realize that you will only get one chance. Concentrate on the bodies below: your body, his body; your skin, his skin. Force them back together one last time.

Just long enough.

Watch him look around the room in surprise. Watch him look down at the body on the bed. Watch him touch the side of his face, skin upon skin. See him smile.

Smile back.

Released.

The Suffering Other

"Start counting backward from ten and by the time you hit five, you won't feel a thing. By the time you hit one, you won't even remember how to count."

Doctor Holborn had probably used that same joke a thousand times without ever realizing it wasn't funny. But having no desire to displease the person about ready to remove a part of her anatomy, Jane laughed anyway.

"Okay, ready? Next thing you know, you'll be waking up tonsil-free."

Ten... nine... eight... seven... six... By the time Jane hit five, she wasn't feeling a thing. By the time she hit one, what happened next made her wish she could forget more than just how to count.

Some people were surgery veterans before they even made it to adulthood—a faulty appendix or a stomach-pumping bout with the drain cleaner. But Jane had gone through almost three decades of life without any major medical glitches, so when she woke up one morning with what felt like a steel collar slapped around her throat, she wrote it off as a spring cold. Three days later, however, after spending the better part of an hour failing to choke down a spoonful of soup, she realized her time had come.

At the hospital, a freshly-scrubbed intern peered into her throat, frowned, and delivered the verdict.

"A very bad case of peritonsillar abscess. We will put you on a course of antibiotics immediately, but the tonsils will most likely have to come out. The sooner the better, in my opinion."

That's how Jane ended up in Dr. Holborn's office deciding how she wanted a part of herself sliced off.

"It's a very simply procedure, which is why a lot of people choose local anesthesia," the doctor told her. "Of course you may also opt for full sedation. It's your choice."

"I just don't want to experience any pain," Jane said.

"Unfortunately, we haven't found a way to stop the body from experiencing pain. But what we can do is convince the *mind* it doesn't *feel* pain. And that works the same with either local anesthesia or full sedation."

"So what's the main difference?"

"The main difference comes down to memory. With I.V. sedation—or what we call 'twilight sedation'—the drugs erase all memory of the operation. Many patients wake up not even realizing the operation is over with."

Jane didn't even like the idea of being on the operating table let alone remembering it. "Twilight sedation it is then."

The green dot went from a steady, predictable blip to a wildly careening Ping-Pong ball more suited to a video game than a heart monitor. Doctor Holborn paused, scalpel frozen in mid-air, and furrowed her brow at the anesthesiologist.

"What's the problem?"

"I'm not sure. Let me adjust the benzodiazepine level."

The anesthesiologist went to work on his arsenal of machines and soon the green dot resumed its placid beep.

"All okay?"

"All okay, doctor. Just a little glitch."

"Let's get this going then," Dr. Holborn said as she lowered the scalpel and made the first cut.

The woman clawing at the ceiling looked familiar, but it was hard to tell. Her face was so contorted and her body so twisted by constant writhing that she hardly even looked human. Not to mention that the woman's skin gave off a deep red glow that quivered and pulsed like an alarm button in a cheesy sci-fi movie.

Jane stared at the pulsing red skin for a long time, but she could discern no pattern. Sometimes the red flashes were fast and intense; sometimes they were slow and subdued.

The writhing woman suddenly curled into a ball and crouched in a corner near the air duct. Jane recognized the Celtic knot tattoo across the small of the woman's back. Right in the middle of the scrollwork were the initials "J.E.R." Her brother liked to joke that if Jane married a man whose last name began with "K," the design would be complete.

Very funny, bro. And since you've always been the older, wise-ass one, maybe you can explain what some scary, discolored version of me is doing rolling around the ceiling of Dr. Holborn's operating room?

Jane was soon sorry she'd asked. As if the pulsing doppelganger had read her mind, the woman suddenly lifted her head and looked at Jane. Actually, since her eyes were rolling in their sockets like a half-mad animal, Jane wasn't sure she was looking *at* her, exactly. But before she had time to figure it out the first wave of pain came and obliterated everything else in the room.

To say that she simply *felt* it would be an injustice. This pain was so enormous, so complete, that it invaded every cell and molecule of her being. A person didn't *feel* pain like that—she *became* it.

Jane opened her mouth to scream, but the drugs had paralyzed her system.

The woman's agony—*her* agony!—was unbearable. Jane was certain she wouldn't survive the next wave when all of a sudden the writhing woman began to flicker in and out of view. The last thing Jane saw was a desperate, pitiful hand reaching out... was she reaching out to *her*, for help?

Jane tried to reach back, but she was still frozen and the woman was fading too fast. The last thing she remembered thinking was how terrible it was to just leave the woman like that, all alone with her pain.

In the recovery room, Jane searched the ceiling as soon as the fog of anesthesia lifted. But of course the woman wasn't there. As she was being wheeled out of post-op, the memory was already becoming as fragmented and intangible as a dream that slips beyond reach the moment after waking up.

At home sipping lemon tea and feeling like someone had taken a cheese grater to her throat, she put the experience down to a drug-induced hallucination, and that was the end of the writhing woman. Or at least Jane thought that was the end.

To the delight of her students, Jane couldn't speak above a whisper for several days, but other than that life quickly returned to normal. She'd been back at work almost a month when the woman returned.

Classes had let out and Jane was in her room catching up on grading. An orange-blossom breeze was drifting through the window, the hallway was alive with the pure joy of recently freed teenagers, and the cleaning crew was getting started in the room next door—in other words, a perfectly ordinary afternoon. That is until her classroom filled with a red glow.

As far as Jane could tell, the woman didn't walk through the door or climb in through the window. She was suddenly just there, filling every inch of space with her writhing, pulsing presence. She looked the same as she had in the operating room—contorted face, eyes rolling back in her head. And just like before, she reached out for Jane. Only this time, instead of extending one arm, she held both out as if offering a rigid embrace.

Jane screamed as the first wave of agonizing pain overtook her, and this time there were no drugs to stop her.

"I'm sorry, but we've run every test available and we can't find anything wrong."

Jane had spent the past three months being poked, prodded, scanned, and turned upside down with her eyes crossed only to be told each time that there was nothing wrong with her. Never mind that she'd had to take an extended sick leave from work; that she only left the house these days when the last pack of instant noodles ran out; and, perhaps worst of all, that her parents were threatening to "come and stay a spell" if she didn't get it together soon. Despite all of that, apparently nothing was wrong.

"The pain started after I got my tonsils out," Jane explained for the hundredth time. "It has to have something to do with that."

The doctor ruffled through Jane's now-thick file and frowned. "You had a very minor reaction to the anesthetics, but that wouldn't cause the problems you claim to be having now."

Claim to be having—how Jane had come to loathe that doctor double-speak!

"The pain is real," she insisted. *And so is the woman*, she wanted to add. But as usual, she left that part out.

The first time the woman appeared in her classroom, Jane wrote it off as post-operation stress, maybe some leftover narcotics in her system. But she showed up again a few weeks later, and now she was quickly becoming Jane's steadiest companion.

She could be ordering coffee at a café or taking a walk around the block, even just hanging out in her apartment watching television or reading a book when the woman would appear. She never spoke, and she never stayed longer than five, ten minutes at the most. The pulsing crimson light and the desperate, outstretched arms never varied, though. Nor did the waves of pain that would paralyze Jane with agony until the woman eventually disappeared as suddenly as she'd come. Sometimes it took hours for her body to feel even close to normal again.

She had learned to stifle the screams. She could even endure the pain now without passing out or calling too much attention to herself. But it was still much easier to stay inside, where she could not only avoid a public scene, but prepare for the writhing woman's return.

This latest doctor's appointment was the first time Jane had been out of her apartment in eight days.

"Perhaps it's time to try a different approach," the doctor said as he scratched something onto a piece of paper and handed it to Jane as he ushered her out the door.

In the solitude of the elevator, she unfolded the paper and saw a referral to Dr. Ruth Jones, psychiatrist in the field of mind-body disorders.

Jane went so far as to make an appointment. She even drove to the clinic and parked her car in the lot. Then she dug her phone out of her bag and canceled the appointment without rescheduling.

She knew the pain was real. In fact, it was the only thing that *was* real any more. Her life had been reduced to either experiencing pain, remembering it, or anticipating it. That was the sneaky thing about pain—before you even knew it, it took over the past, present, and future all in one go.

If Jane's doppelganger existed only in her head, no psychiatrist could help her. If she was real, only one person could eliminate her—the original version who for some unimaginable reason had conjured her into being in the first place.

Having given up on doctors, Jane turned to the Internet, the next best source of medical misinformation. In less than an hour, she'd found over a dozen sites on out-of-body experiences during surgery, strange and threatening encounters with doppelgangers, and a support group for sufferers of chronic psychic pain. But none mentioned that hypnotic crimson pulsing.

She ran a few more searches and was about to give up when she found it: a simple page with none of the usual images, ads, bells or whistles. Just pages and pages of entries and a simple title at the top: The Suffering Other

Jane started with the most recent entry, dated Monday, July 16, 2012:

> He came at dawn. I can't believe I never connected it before, but I finally figured out the pattern. That awful, awful light slows down and speeds up and grows brighter and dimmer in perfect synchronicity with the beating of my own heart.

She read a few more pages and wasn't surprised to find that every entry chronicled a pain-wracked visit from a pulsing red man. Now and then an entry would catch her eye with some new piece of a diabolical puzzle that seemed to have no discernible endpoint or design:

Tuesday, March 22, 2011

It has been over a year now since I've taken so much as an aspirin for a headache. I no longer visit the doctor because I dread the discovery of some ailment that would require surgery. It is my hope that if I cannot make him go away, at least I can help alleviate his suffering. So far the experiment does not seem to be working.

Wednesday, February 25, 2009

Yesterday I was ready. As soon as he appeared, I plugged in the iron. When it was hot enough, I pressed the tip against my forearm and held it there as long as I could stand. My theory was that by inducing extreme pain in his presence, I could fix whatever disrupted equilibrium made him appear. But it seemed to have no impact on him whatsoever. Just like always, the pain came right before he disappeared, only now I also had the pain from the hot iron. One more experiment failed.

The farther back Jane went the more normal the entries became—references to a wife and two daughters that suddenly vanished; an accounting job that must have gone by the wayside along with them; a life full of activity that the pulsing man, who the writer called "The Suffering Other," had slowly reduced to these lifeless lines of pain.

Four hours and two bleary eyes later, Jane reached the first entry, dated Saturday, May 19, 2007:

I started this blog because of something weird that's been happening to me (so strangers on the Internet can think I'm crazy instead of my wife!). Anyway, this whole thing started about three months ago when I was out horseback riding. I'll skip the details, but I took a spill and ended up with a mess of broken bones and a smack on the head bad enough to cause me to start going in and out of consciousness. I guess I was going into shock, but before I lost consciousness altogether I saw this weird version of myself kind of hovering in the air above me trying to grab at me or something. Only this 'other me' was kind of glowing red and he was twisting around like he was in terrible pain. Then all of a sudden I was in pain, too, a worse kind of pain than I've ever felt in my whole life. I guess I must have passed out for good, because fast forward and I was in the hospital recovering. I basically forgot about the weird floating guy once I got out, but—and this is the weird part, folks!—a few weeks later I had a vision or a hallucination of the same red glowing man. Worse yet I felt the same kind of pain again. I swear I don't do any drugs, and as far as I know I'm not crazy! (Though my kids might say otherwise). The "other me" has been back four times now, and it's starting to get kind of difficult to deal with. My doctor thinks maybe it's some effect from the head injury but so far the tests haven't turned up anything. I guess I'm hoping someone out there might have had a similar experience and can help me out about what's going on and what I can do about it. Thanks, Dave.

Jane stared at the screen so long the words began to blur, but one thing remained perfectly, terrifyingly clear: the Suffering Other had been visiting this poor man for *five years*… and he wasn't showing any signs of going away.

It took two months before Jane finally tracked Dave down. There hadn't been a contact email on the site, so she'd broken her self-imposed exile and called her most tech-savvy friend. Luckily, he was also the least likely to ask why she was calling him out of the blue asking for the contact information of a complete stranger.

Dave lived in Silver Creek, Nebraska, and at first it never occurred to her to show up on his doorstep like a lunatic stalker. When her first three emails went unanswered she decided to let the whole thing go. But then something happened that put talking to Dave at the top of her priority list.

She'd been crouched in her living room hoping that whoever was knocking on her door would think she wasn't home. After that first slip-up with the rent she'd been careful to at least pay the bills on time, so no one should have been stopping by for a visit.

When the knocking finally stopped Jane rose from her hiding place just as the room filled with the familiar pulsing red light. Jane braced herself and waited for the tsunami waves of pain to wash over her. Only this time, once they had receded, the woman did not simply disappear. This time the reaching arms with the bony hands and long, delicate fingers—*her* fingers, *her* hands!—finally found their target.

Red-hot fire raged through Jane's body and then froze her into an icy stasis even more unbearable than the heat.

I can't move, I'm frozen forever within this pain.

That was the last thing Jane remembered before she lost consciousness. Only later when she caught sight of herself in the bathroom mirror did the full memory of what happened return to her. On each shoulder was an angry red blister in the shape of an outstretched hand.

By six o'clock that same evening, Jane was on a plane to Silver Creek, Nebraska.

The dilapidated trailer looked abandoned, but Jane knew that was probably its inhabitant's intent. She edged closer to the door and peered down at a row of little piles arranged neatly in front of the world's most misplaced "Welcome" mat. One of the piles revealed a skinned mouse carcass, its forlorn tail connected to a tiny pile of intestines. Another looked like what might have once been a shrew, only with its head missing, Jane couldn't be sure.

The bile rose in her throat and she ducked behind a blighted goldenrod bush to force it down. The executioner soon revealed itself in the form of a sly-eyed tabby cat that slunk around the side of the trailer and sat there contemplating Jane's potential as the next sacrifice to the doormat gods.

She must have proven an unworthy offering, because the cat strolled over and rubbed along the side of her leg in cautious greeting.

Unless Dave had unusually morbid taste in lawn ornaments, the corpses indicated that he hadn't been outside in some time. Jane knew from her own recent habits that a knock on the door would probably go unanswered. Yet even the most forlorn and forsaken crave a little companionship now and then—in Dave's case, Jane figured Tom-cat here was it.

She crouched down and let out what she hoped was her most authentic cat-in-distress yowl.

The cat shot off into the weeds and, sure enough, the front door soon cracked open. A tentative voice called through the screen, "Tazzy?"

Jane knew she would have only once chance. She stepped out from behind the goldenrod and said, "I think my Suffering Other is trying to kill me."

Every inch of the narrow living room was filled with stacks of magazines, piles of books, and scatterings of pictures, articles, and images cut, torn, and printed from a vast and seemingly random array of sources. Competing for the limited floor and shelf space were crumpled junk food bags, empty cracker boxes, and dishes congealed with grease. Whereas Jane's Suffering Other had caused her to lose interest in food entirely, Dave's had apparently had the reverse effect.

After gesturing for her to follow him inside, Dave molded himself into a reclining chair where he now sat as silent and immovable as a mountain, a human kingdom of flesh surrounded by a moat of debris and detritus.

Jane recounted her story in a rush of words, but Dave remained silent. She wasn't even sure he'd been listening until one word finally emerged from the mountain-king: "Fascinating."

He sat there letting the silence regroup before finally adding, "My Suffering Other never touched me. For a while I tried every way I could think of to try and touch him, but I could never even get close."

"What do you think is happening?" Jane asked. "I've read your blog, I know what's *happening*, but..." Even though Jane had been determined to talk to the only person in the world who understood what she'd been going through, she realized she had no idea what she expected him to say.

"*Why* is this happening?" she tried again.

"A trauma so great that it can't be absorbed," Dave said. "At least not all at once. So it gets cast out of time, cast out of consciousness. It's still happening, though, and that's where things get tricky."

"And this kind of... trauma cast out of time," Jane said, trying to follow along. "This is where the Suffering Other comes from?" It occurred to her, not for the first time, that Dave might be insane. But then what did that make her?

"Theory used to be that human consciousness was a unified system," he said. "But now the thinking is that it's more like a mirror— one smooth surface right up until we struggle for our very first breath of independent air. And then the mirror *shatters!*" Dave clapped his hands together and Jane jumped at the unexpected show of life in his otherwise inert body. "After that it keeps on shattering into endless splinters with each new rock thrown at it. And pain is one very big fucking rock."

Dave gestured toward a stack of books next to his chair with a wave of one meaty, once-again listless hand. Jane noticed a scar on his left forearm in the unmistakable shape of a hot iron's tip.

"I used to read a lot of medical journals, although recently I've turned to philosophy."

"So you're saying our pain somehow caused the Suffering Others to take on a consciousness of their own?" Jane asked.

"I'm saying that abolishing the *feeling* of pain is not the same thing as the abolishing pain *itself*," Dave said, echoing Dr. Holborn's explanation about anesthesia. "It has to go somewhere. It's like flushing shit down the toilet thinking it just disappears. But it ends up somewhere. Same thing with pain."

When Jane taught her students about the American Civil War, she used an anthology of first-person narratives that included an almost unreadable account of doctors performing operations on unanesthesized patients. One of her best friends in high school had been in a car accident that left him with nerve damage so severe that only constantly adjusted medication made it bearable.

"But human beings are not meant to suffer pain the way we did before modern medical advances. There's no way I believe we're meant to suffer like that."

"Who knows what's meant to be," Dave said. "But the pain still has to go somewhere."

"Then why doesn't everyone have a Suffering Other?"

Dave shifted in his chair and looked directly at her for the first time. "Who's saying they don't?"

When Jane didn't answer, he said, "If you want my opinion—and that's why you're here, right?—there are countless Suffering Others out there. Maybe infinite. But we're obviously not meant to see them. Or at least remember them."

"Why do some of us remember?" Jane asked.

"I don't know. Something goes wrong somewhere. Something breaks through whatever barrier separates us. And we see them."

Jane thought about the "mild reaction" she'd had to the anesthesia. It turns out it hadn't been so mild after all.

"And once we've seen them," Jane made herself say, "once we're aware that they exist—they want us to share some of the burden."

"I'm not sure what they want," Dave said. "I'm not sure about anything much anymore."

"Do you know of any others who have seen them?"

"Only two I ever came across before I stopped wanting to know, though there must be more out there. The first was a guy in England I only heard from once. His Suffering Other came to him during a bad reaction he had to the anti-depressants he was taking after his wife died."

"How does that relate to the pain concept?"

"Pain doesn't just include physical."

No, I guess not," Jane said. "What about the second person?"

"That was a woman from Thailand. I didn't hear from her directly. A member of her family contacted me after reading my blog. Last I heard they had to put her in an institution after she tried to jump out the window of a ten story building."

Jane was about to speak when the listless hand stopped her.

"You might as well not even ask me how to get rid of them," Dave said. "If there is an answer, you can see for yourself I haven't found it yet."

The last of the pain pills were gone and Jane wasn't sure what to do. She'd lost her health insurance months ago, and even if she could find a new doctor there was no way she'd get another prescription. The parking lot of Magic's and the underpass on Fifth Street were always reliable pharmaceutical alternatives, but the money had run out along with the pills. She wasn't ready to pursue the remaining options, but give it a couple more days and all bets were off.

Last month she'd moved out of her apartment into a one room monthly in order to save on rent. The school didn't have her new address and her leave of absence had come and gone, but she wouldn't be returning to work anyway. With no phone, no forwarding address, and no plans to change that situation, Jane had learned that the true definition of freedom was the inability to be summoned.

Her Suffering Other, though, seemed to have her own tracking system.

Before she'd left Nebraska, Jane had asked Dave to recount all of his experiments. She'd read about them on his blog, but she needed to hear the results directly from him—he had found no way to get rid of the Suffering Other or the pain that came with it.

On the plane ride back to California, Jane reasoned that if her Suffering Other could touch her, then unlike Dave, she might be able to touch her back. And that's when Jane had made up her mind to kill her Suffering Other.

It had seemed a simple enough plan, but whenever the time came, Jane's courage would waver. After that first time, the Suffering Other had never tried to embrace her again, so it just seemed easier to endure her rather than take the chance of trying to destroy her. After all, she was a part of Jane, wasn't she?

The opiates made that decision much easier—the drugs didn't completely take the pain away, but close enough.

But now the pills were gone.

Jane picked up the carving knife she kept by the mattress on the floor. With no more pills, no more money, and no more options, she would just lie down and wait. This time, her courage could not fail.

By the time the pulsing crimson light broke through the haze of Jane's half-sleep, the room was slipping into the darkness of a moonless night. Jane sat up and secured her grip on the knife. It was a vicious-looking thing, its seven-inch blade flat on one side and curved to a lethal point on the other.

"Come on," she whispered. "It's time to end this thing once and for all."

Jane didn't know if it was possible to kill the Suffering Other, and she didn't know what would happen if she tried. She only knew that one way or the other, it had to end. She didn't want to be a shadow-person wasting away behind locked doors, waiting for the day when she would jump out the window of a ten-story building.

The Suffering Other reached out her arms and moved closer. Jane held the knife against the side of her leg. The woman's constantly rolling rabid-dog eyes always made it hard to tell what she was looking at, if anything, but Jane wasn't taking any chances.

She was right in front of her now. The pulses of light were coming fast, like a crimson strobe light. Jane got a mental fix on the woman's chest and closed her eyes. She knew that if she looked at her, she'd never be able to do it.

The knife struck its target and stopped midway. Her eyes wide open now, Jane drove it forward with all her remaining strength. It slid all the way in, and Jane let go.

The woman stepped backward. She seemed unconcerned about the knife handle jutting from her chest. Her eyes were now clear and sharp, and for the first time since she'd appeared to Jane her body was still.

The Suffering Other stared at Jane, and Jane stared back at her.

The light pulses were very slow now. Soon it would be too dark to see anything. Jane watched in fascination as the woman's familiar mask of agony transformed into something so unexpected that it took a moment to realize what had changed—in the last faint flickers of crimson, Jane saw the Suffering Other smile.

The family had been calling the coroner's office every day and Dr. Newman still hadn't finished the paperwork. Of course they wanted to bury their daughter, and they had every right to do so. But his name would be on the death certificate, not theirs, and for that to happen he had to be sure. Sometimes, though, there was just no way to be sure, and this was one of those times.

The problem wasn't the cause of death. There was no question about the carving knife buried to the hilt in the middle of the woman's chest. The problem was how and why it had ended up there.

Suicide by stabbing was unusual, but not unheard of. The victim did have a drug problem and a recent history of erratic behavior. Her emaciated body bore the familiar signs of someone reaching the end of a long downward spiral.

If her final facial expression was anything to go on, at least she'd found a bit of peace at the end. It was hard to tell with the dead, but it looked to Dr. Newman like she might have even been smiling.

Even so, the angle of the knife wound was all wrong for a suicide. According to forensics it could have been self-inflicted, but very unlikely unless Jane Reynolds had been a double-jointed acrobat. Yet the crime scene report said the door and window of the apartment had been locked with no signs of tampering.

Dr. Newman pressed the extension number for his assistant.

"Listen, Carol, could you give the Reynolds family a call and tell them the body will be ready for release on Wednesday? Oh, and leave a message for Detective Chang in homicide to call me as soon as she gets a chance."

The section of the death certificate meant to record any cause of death other than natural was still blank. Titled "Death Due to External Violence," it included four choices: homicide, suicide, accident, and undetermined.

The doctor lingered one last time before checking "Undetermined." Maybe he hadn't been able to figure out exactly what had happened to Jane Erin Reynolds, but that "undetermined" in the death certificate at least left open the possibility that someday someone else might.

"Until then," he said, closing the file, "at least she's no longer suffering."

A Simple Game of Chess

It has been three-hundred and sixty-two days, four and one-half hours since I last saw the shadowed hollow with the twisted tree, that cursed place that haunts my every minute—every second!—in both waking hours and sleep no longer fit for dreams. Everywhere I look—even in this horrid place of beige walls and beige floors and beige faces—I see those tattered leaves fleeing from moss-covered branches; that forest floor fetid and alive with crawling ferns and reaching brambles; and most of all, that crooked, devilish tree with the twisted, grasping arms, the trunk so deformed with gnarls that a hundred malevolent faces seem to seethe in wait for the unsuspecting wanderer.

Tell me, how could one not come to an evil end in such a place?

How could one—but wait! I hear them coming, and they must not catch me writing in this again. I must hide it under the mattress and pretend to sleep—

Oh, they are so easily fooled, these beige faces! It is quiet now in the hallway, the moon my only companion. The night is peaceful save for the moans and cries that punctuate each and every night in this living museum of malfunction and woe. Occasionally I still wake at night believing that I am in my own master bedroom, on sheets of the finest Egyptian cotton. Then the sickly moon casts its pallor over the peeling walls and grime-patterned floor and my mind cries out, *My God! How did I end up in such a dreadful place?*

The shadowed hollow with the twisted tree never fails to remind me.

It was not easy to drag him there, not in the least! It's true that he is—or should I say *was*, ha-ha, how forgetful of me!—a small, slight man. But the hollow is remote and the forest thick, his stiffening corpse most uncooperative despite the tarp and, if I may say so myself, the ingeniously devised pulling-ropes I fashioned just for the occasion. By the time we reached our destination I was entirely spent—he, on the other hand, was none the worse for wear, ha-ha! My exhaustion no doubt accounts for the peculiar fact that at first I didn't even notice the tree. Only hours later, when I could stand knee deep in the grave, did I chance to look up and see the horrid faces supervising each shovelful of overturned earth.

How those faces haunt me! The one with the tongue sticking out in a lewd jest; another looking like an angry pontiff shaking an accusing finger, his peaked cap dipping forward to meet his long, craven chin. But it was the one with the sly leer that drew my gaze again and again. Its mouth was turned up at one corner in a deliberate perversion of a smile, its left eye squinted into a knowing wink. Was it winking at *me*? What did it know to make it so bawdy and mocking?

As I gazed up at that degenerate tree-face, for the first time I began to question the rectitude of my deed. But surely he had wronged me one too many times! Surely he had deserved to die!

Seized by panic, I rushed to the tarp and tore back the clips holding it closed. There was the same face, still handsome even with the first fingers of decay probing the features—and, more maddening yet, still that same self-satisfied expression, as imperturbable in death as in life!

More than anything else it was that expression which drove me back to my labor, back to the hole that would forever seal that villainous face from the world! No, the tree was not scolding me, was not mocking me for my folly. Rather, I thought, the tree was winking at me as if to say, "We are in on this together, you and I!"

The tree was a complicit witness to this most secret burial ceremony. The gnarled roots would act as pallbearers, the clumps of fetid forest growth would form unwritten tombstones for this most lonely of graves.

After all, I reassured myself, I had not been the one to provoke him. Oh, no, I had done nothing but seek his praise; week after week, month after month, vying for his attention like a pitiful schoolboy. It sickens me even now to think of the hours I sat crafting ways to draw him toward me, the countless nights spent pining for even one message, one small sign that he cared of my existence at all.

The horrid *disgrace* of it all—why, my family had been commanding estates and nations while his were still tilling the fields for a scrap of frozen potato! And yet always that maddening, impenetrable gaze; always those full, lewd lips that never granted a smile or a friendly word. How many messages ignored, how many overtures shunned before any man must choose between either his self-control or his self-respect?

I admit, the fatal arrow was prepared by my hand—but it was dipped into poison by his. Oh, yes, I remember it well! One of those merciless parties with endlessly revolving displays of importance—kiss-kiss, smile-smile, all the while each grinning rictus secretly wishing to smash into atoms the head of the mirror-image rictus grinning back! He had been in a corner of the room—surrounded by fawning sycophants, naturally!—with that bemused air I so despise. I watched and waited. When he was finally alone, I took my opportunity.

"Ha-ha," I said, my laugh mildly ironic, knowing. "You must not have gotten my message yesterday. Empty inbox again this morning, ha-ha!"

He paused for what seemed to me a very long time, and then said, "It went a bit late last night, so I ended up sleeping most of the day away."

It went a bit late? Did he imagine that I knew to what *it* he was referring? I, who obviously had not been invited to this marvelous *it* that had absorbed an entire night and half day of his life?

He was looking at me strangely with those heavy-lidded eyes that always seemed to suggest something salacious and obscene. I saw that he expected an answer even though he had asked me no question. I became acutely aware of a thin layer of sweat filming my forehead.

"Oh, ha-ha!," I said, again relying upon the ironic laugh. "Such decadence!"

That maddening pause again. Who could be expected to retain an ounce of restraint in the face of such a man? Then he said the words that sealed his fate the very seconds it took to utter them:

"Today more or less all left Communists hold that a theory of decadence is necessary in order to be a Marxist."

My eyes must have widened at this remark, for how could they not? Was he mocking me, this arrogant fool? Challenging my knowledge of political theory? Ridiculing my inherited fortune in the face of his much larger earned one?

Did any genuine Marxists even *exist* these days?

I ask you, what could any man be expected to do in a situation such as this? What man could stand in the face of such impudence and not feel the first splinters in the smiling mask that conceals the true face beneath?

I laughed again and remarked on the late hour. The next thing I knew I was back in the safety of my own den before a cheerful fire, sipping my brandy and planning his murder.

I plotted and fantasized for many months before I acted. I had read all of the grand old stories many, many times. I knew just what to do and precisely how to do it. To be sure, I didn't possess a rare cask of Amontillado, but I knew his tastes well—always the connoisseur, always the gentleman! A rare and exquisite 1998 Reserve pinot, shared over a simple game of chess, would serve my purposes splendidly.

Patient reader, I shall spare you the details of my casual yet cunning proposal; the greedy lust that stole into his eyes at my reference to the wine's vintage; the lascivious, full lips curving upward in what on any other man I would call a smile. I fully confess to the intoxicating thrill of knowing that finally—finally!—*I* possessed something that *he* should covet so fiercely!

I shall spare you the details of how I calmly waited for him that evening in the den; how, lacking a wine cellar and even a hint of masonry skills, I simply cleaved his head in with a fire poker, stashed his still-warm body in the trunk of my fuel-efficient car, and drove to the farthest edge of the farthest forest I could find. A simple, perfect plan— perfect in its very simplicity!—if only I had known of the wicked tree that awaited me in that hollow.

Wait—is that the sun struggling through those grimy squares of morning misery? Yes, there is the cursed buzzer—Pavlov's dogs to the dining hall, march, march, march! I must hide this under the mattress, for if they find it again I will be punished. Oh, I am a bad, bad boy indeed!

The horrors of this place, where a man must endure day after day of mindless routine, endless scrutiny, ceaseless charade—simply to steal away a few precious moments with his own thoughts. The worst sort of hell imaginable, not even owning one's own imagination. Now where was I? And what time is it?

Three-hundred and sixty-*three* days, five and one-quarter hours. Getting closer, ever closer! But I must not get ahead of myself. Must not rush things and get out of order.

Not a soul suspected me when he failed to turn up for his endless rounds of meetings and social events. And why should they— me, a mere footnote in his vast and impressive networks; me, who was nothing to him. Mysterious disappearance! Unaccountable absence! Inexplicable evaporation! How delicious those first months were as I sat by the fire, sipping my pinot and chuckling at my own cleverness.

"Decadence, indeed," I often said. "Here's a toast to decadence!"

It was in the sixth month that I first dreamed of the hollow. I could somehow see beneath the earth where he slumbered in the worm-infested bed I had prepared for him, covered in a blanket of slime-blackened leaves and creeping vines. I saw, even more vividly than before, the treacherous tree-faces leering down in voyeuristic violation of his eternal rest. Even more horrifying, I saw the tree's lustful roots penetrating downward to perform despicable acts upon his body.

I woke with a strangled scream that echoed through the halls and outward toward the waiting forest.

After that, the tree visited nightly. Each time it crept deeper into my senses and took further hold of my soul. The cool, smooth cotton sheets transformed into tree bark capable of tormenting my skin into red, livid welts. The silk blankets became entangling branches holding me fast in suffocating embrace. The faces winked and leered in depraved amusement at my helplessness.

Before long, my waking moments grew just as tormented as my dreams. Neither the garish light of day nor the subdued shadows of evening could banish the tree and its hundred fiendish faces.

By the twelfth month I knew that I must return to the hollow or be driven to irrevocable madness. I knew that I must once again turn my fevered gaze upward to that twisted, Janus-faced tree. I knew—of course I knew!—that I must dig up the grave and confess the evil deed as my own.

Death would unite us in a way that life had never allowed!

It took some doing before those stony-faced police people took me seriously—so suspicious, so reluctant to believe! But I convinced them with details only the guilty could possess. I remembered everything, down to the color and material of the last shirt he wore—green, silk-cotton blend! You can imagine, my dear reader, how horrid that trip back to the shadowed hollow was—the forest whispering and laughing on all sides; the dogs and police people tromping ahead, intruders on this unsacred ground. For one desperate moment I almost professed the entire thing a morbid joke, almost begged to turn around and go back to my study to sip brandy and laugh at my own foolishness!

But the tree, I knew, would follow me anywhere I tried to flee from its all-seeing eyes.

With each step closer my heart fluttered with dread, my soul tingled with terror. At last we reached the fearful spot. At last I realized that the tree was not witness to my crime, but prosecutor.

"I confess!" I shouted at my ancient accuser. "Overturn the foul soil and unearth the equally foul evidence of my treachery!"

Oh, those police already thought me mad as they dug up the place where the earth was still unnaturally fresh even after so much time. They dug deeper and deeper—far deeper than I ever did—and when they found nothing, they dug some more. Hole after hole, deeper and wider, until finally the hollow was nothing but mounds of empty, overturned earth.

All the while, the tree-faces leered and winked—a most complicit witness after all.

What wicked trickery was at work in that hollow? Had this fiendish tree somehow *moved* his body like a gruesome, rotting pawn in a diabolical chess game devised by the devil himself?

I looked up at the tree in helpless terror. That's when I saw that a new face had been added to the already over-abundant display of perversity: its heavy-lidded eyes seemed to suggest something salacious and obscene; its full, lewd lips never granted a smile or a friendly word. That self-satisfied expression, that maddening, impenetrable gaze was now frozen forever in the pitiless tree that would haunt my soul and torment my mind until the end of my days.

"It has taken him!" I shrieked, pointing at the tree. "Look, you fools, at the faces!"

They winked and leered more profanely than ever, pleased to let me in on their wicked game. The police people, however, did not share in the amusement.

For days on end I lay in a stupor of despair. I neglected my personal and household duties and turned every visitor away from my doorstep. Only when I hit upon an idea so obvious and yet so previously obscure did I stir from my bed chamber for the first time in months: if the laws governing whatever infernal world had created the tree allowed it to steal his soul, certainly the laws of *this* world dictated that his *body* must still be somewhere upon it. If I could find the body and remove it from that cursed place, perhaps I could break the tree's hold upon *my* soul, even if his was condemned forever to that abominable tapestry of gnarled bark.

A simple game of chess, you see, and I had devised a most cunning check mate indeed!

I lost count of the times I ventured to that forsaken hollow, of how many holes I dug over and over again only to find empty earth. Each time I set out with new purpose and determination; each time I returned in defeated despair.

My descent into degenerate decay continued. When the knock came that signaled the arrival of those who had long wished to drag me from my home and rob me of my freedom, I was not in the least bit surprised.

What's that you say? That I somehow had the wrong spot? And yet how could I not know that spot—the very one that haunts my every moment, whose every detail is pressed upon my soul by the devil's own branding iron? No, even if I live to an age where both reason and memory fail me, I could rise from my dying slumber and go directly to that shadowed hollow, straight to that leering tree without one misstep.

Well, then, the rational reader might say, perhaps you did not really kill him; perhaps the pinot had gone to your head, had altered your senses beyond reason. Did not really kill him, you say? With such imaginative powers, perhaps *you* should be the teller of tales, not I! Propose such a story to these same hands that scrubbed his brain matter out of my best woolen rug, the one carefully handed down through seven ancestral generations; explain your theory to the hands torn open by forest brambles that tried to claim his tarp-wrapped carcass as their own—the same hands that covered him with shovelful after shovelful of black, dank earth full of the very worms and beetles that would soon feast upon his now-finished flesh.

Oh, I see it plainly! You think me as mad as these infuriating doctors whose smiles form such poor camouflage for their contemptuous eyes. Ah, but the tree and I shall have the last laugh, for I have not been spending these—wait, what time is it now?—I have not been spending these three-hundred and sixty-three days, three and one-half hours idly. I know just the latch on just the bathroom window that never catches properly, and just how far it is from the ledge to the ground. I have watched the beige-faces every second of every day. I know just the hour when one is most likely to sneak into an empty room to catch up on lost sleep. I know just the moment when the one left alone at the night desk has let his attention stray a little too far.

The carving knife secreted away from the kitchen and hidden deep within my mattress these long months is now ready to open the throat of any man foolish enough to get in the way of another man's destiny.

Three-hundred and sixty-three days, three and one-quarter hour. Almost time for one last game of chess.

Rest assured, I have two secret weapons to aid me against this most formidable foe. The first is the kind of human single-mindedness which the placidly timeless tree cannot even begin to imagine. The second is an even more substantial product of human determination— the freshly sharpened, long-handled ax I took care to bury the last time I visited the hollow. I knew even then of their scheming plans to lock me within these horrid beige walls—little did *they* know that I had already begun formulating a plan of my own.

The fools, to think they could outmaneuver the tree so easily! There are only two participants in this contest—the tree, and the one who must defeat it or die in the attempt.

But a tree that plays too many tricks may discover that there is more than one way to finish a match.

Chop-chop, make haste! If I act quickly, I can make it to the hollow by morning. Perhaps the tree will finally return his body to the one who put it there; perhaps I will finally be allowed to take my place beside him in death as never granted in life.

I must say goodbye now, for either way I shall not be returning to these beige walls ever again. Whatever the outcome, the tree and I will make our final moves.

No stalemates permitted, and only the earth to which all players must eventually return shall be crowned chess master of this endgame.

Checkmate, indeed!

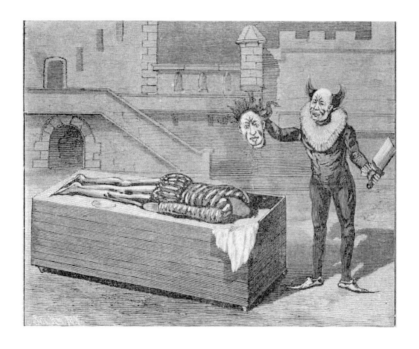

The Devil's in the Details

For what must have been the hundredth time in the past twelve hours, Maz turned a full circle in the middle of the uneven little orbit of road. He scanned the flat horizon, but for the hundredth time saw only the same jaundice-yellow fields of scrub.

"God-*damn* leave offa my neck!" Maz slapped away a huge horsefly so persistent it put even New York City cockroaches to shame. Roaches or no, Maz wished he was back in Brooklyn right now, hanging with the band at the Hi-Low instead of spinning around in the middle of a delta backwater being eaten alive by mutant insects.

If the devil was hanging around somewhere in Clarksdale, Mississippi, waiting for a soul to steal, this burned-out stretch of fly-paper wasn't it.

He'd been out here since last night and all through the stifling hot next day. The last of his food and water were gone and now another evening was coming on. Not a single car had gone by the whole time, and Maz could see why. Nobody would risk busting an axle on these rutted-out dirt roads even if they could find them—there hadn't been a stop sign or road marker the entire two mile drive from the edge of town to the place where the four roads met and intersected.

The Crossroads—the place Robert Johnson had supposedly traded off his soul to the devil in order to be the greatest blues player that ever lived. The place Mathew "Maz" Zolbe had spent nine-hundred and nine dollars plus expenses to fly over a thousand miles to do the same. All of which was now looking like the exact waste of time and money Laurid always said it would be.

"That's just a story thought up to make somethin' out of nothin'," she'd said after Maz had once again brought up the idea of someday standing in that legendary patch of road. They were in the middle of a rehearsal, and maybe it was on his mind because the band had just landed their first gig at The Bowery. They had it on good word that some major label scouts would be in the audience. Sweet Tonic had played every back alley club in the city for the past three years, often for less money than the cost of the gas it took to haul their gear across town. They'd attracted some solid critical attention and had built a decent fan base, but lately the whole thing was starting to feel like pissing in the harbor all pleased with your little contribution to the great big Atlantic, and then noticing a thousand other guys alongside you with their joints hanging out all doing the exact same thing.

But this show at The Bowery could change all that. And since Maz was not only the singer and lead guitar player but the front-and-center soul of the whole band, it was up to him more than anyone else to make that happen.

"Isn't that what music's all about, though?" Maz had asked no one in particular.

"What, making money and scoring women?" Ethan said.

"Even if you did the first it wouldn't help with the second," Laurid shot back.

"No, I mean music, that's what it's all about," Maz tried again. "Making something out of nothing. Conjuring a little magic so people can stand all the otherwise ordinary shit in their lives."

Ravi blapped out a flat note on his saxophone. "Sounds like the *black* kind of magic you're talkin' 'bout," he said. "I wouldn't sell my soul to nobody, no how."

"Nobody would want your raggedy-ass soul," Ethan yelled from behind his drum kit, and everybody dissolved into laughter.

"Let's pick it up at the chorus," Laurid said. "The only magic we need to be thinkin' about is this damn time change."

But Maz keep thinking about Robert Johnson just the same as he struggled to get that sound, that *just right* something that could send the music straight out of your skin and all the way through the roof and into the stratosphere and back down again. That something sets an artist on fire the first time he or she finds it, and every single one chases after it for the rest of their lives. But most never even get close, not even the good ones. Only a very lucky few get that kind of juice, and Maz was beginning to think he wasn't one of them.

Unlike the rest of the band, though, Maz thought it was more than worth selling your soul for. The way he figured it, any musician worth a damn sells his or her soul anyway, often with nothing more to show for it than an empty bottle of booze and a bank account to match. If the devil made you the best in the business and then came calling a little earlier than expected, well, that was still more than a fair deal as far as Maz was concerned. The music would live forever anyway, and that's all that mattered.

Maz had probably been ready to make that trade-off the first time he'd heard about the Crossroads from Old Lady Ivy.

Nobody knew how old Ivy was, but she'd been old as long as Maz had known her. She lived in the apartment next door and watched Maz after school until his mom got home from work. Ol' Ivy could pick a mean guitar herself, which is probably why she'd been the first to spot the talent in Maz.

"You got the music in you," she'd tell him. "But you'd best leave that guitar alone, son. Ain't no future in it but an early grave." And she should know, because her old man had just up and left her one day to seek his fortunes with a slow-eyed hussy named Yodelin' Barb.

"Just took off one day and never seen hides or tails of him since. Includin' no billboard at the Apollo with him and that yodelin' hussy's names on it, neither."

Even better than Yodelin' Barb, though, were Old Lady Ivy's stories about the mysterious place known to Maz in those days only as "The South," where Ivy had spent her childhood before leaving home for the cold-hustle cities of the North.

"Things is different down there," she'd say. "Deep and dark and sweet, just like the land."

One day she'd stood there kneading bread into little balls and told Maz the story of Robert Johnson and the Crossroads.

"Back in the nineteen-twenties, Mr. Johnson wanted more than anything else in the world to play the blues. Thing is, he couldn't play half as good as he wanted to. That was all right as long as he had his sweet wife around to make up for what the music wouldn't give him. But after she went and died tryin' to bring their child into the world, Mr. Johnson didn't care for nothing no more except the music. Only thing is, though, he still wasn't any good at it.

"When Mr. Johnson disappeared one day, folks thought he'd finally gone and drank himself to death on moonshine. But he turned up again, only now he could play that guitar like all the angels and demons of heaven and hell both had come together in one wailin' crazy hallelujah chorus. Mr. Johnson would sit all night long in the graveyard, right on top of the tombstones, raisin' the very dead outta the ground with that guitar."

Old Lady Ivy dropped her voice to a whisper and Maz had to lean in close to hear her.

"Nothin' could account for such a change, and that's what got people talkin' 'bout how Mr. Johnson had gone down to the Crossroads just before midnight when the devil rides. The devil promised to tune Mr. Johnson's guitar with the fires of hell itself in exchange for his eternal soul. Well, don't you know that fool went and took the deal? Only the devil, being the devil that he is, done cheated Mr. Johnson by comin' for his soul before that poor man had even gotten his proper due. Now, the devil knew once word got out what happened, no one was ever gonna take a deal like that again, so from then on he made sure them poor fools had all kinds of fame and riches before he come to take their souls."

In that tiny kitchen surrounded by the earthy smell of rising yeast, Maz had pictured the devil pulling up to the crossroads in a great big red Cadillac with a beautiful woman by his side and a lacquered red guitar stashed in the back seat. Although he didn't know it yet, that afternoon a seed had been planted that would take another fourteen years to take root and come to flower.

Or to rise up and strangle him like a poison vine, depending on your point of view.

As soon as the band had gotten the gig at The Bowery, Maz had known the time had come to find out once and for all if the Crossroads was more than just a story. He'd booked a flight to Mississippi without telling anyone, and now here he was, sweating through his silk shirt about ready to pass out from dehydration.

Determined as he was to flush out the devil, even Maz knew when the time had come to give up. He slammed the rental car back toward town so fast the gravel flew out behind him like a shotgun blast. The sun was just beginning a lazy descent when he realized he'd passed the same farmhouse three times in a row.

He pulled into the sun-scorched field in front of the dilapidated house. He was about to pull up the useless map that had gotten him lost in the first place when he saw the old man perched high up on a stool on the sagging back porch.

Most of the old man's face was in the shadow of a battered black cowboy hat pulled down low across his forehead, but his bent and withered body told his age just the same.

"That old-timer's got to know the way back to town," Maz muttered as he started across the field. "Was prob'ly sitting on that same stool before there even *was* a town."

As Maz got closer he saw that the old man was picking the strings of what looked to be a wartime Gibson flat-top. Those suckers went back to the 1940s and were made with what many regarded as an almost mythical combination of materials, some of which didn't even exist anymore. They sold for as high as ten-thousand dollars if you could even find one, and this old dude was just banging away on his like it was any old pawn shop special.

Dude didn't even look like he could afford his next hot meal let alone a fine instrument like that—

Maz stopped dead in his tracks right in the middle of the field. A man with a guitar like that in a place like this probably knew exactly how to scare up the devil. This was the South, after all—maybe all Maz needed was a proper introduction.

The old man didn't even look up from his playing when Maz approached.

"I came out this way looking for something and got kind of lost," Maz said. "I was hopin' you could help me find it."

"Depends what you came into the Delta lookin' for whether or not I can help you find it," the old man said, still not looking up from his picking.

It killed Maz the way people around here talked about coming "into" the Delta—not *to* the Delta, but *into* it, as if traveling back in time to some separate world of its own.

The smell of hickory smoke and frying catfish drifted out of an open window. All of a sudden Maz wanted to just ask for directions and leave like any sane person would do. What if this dude was just some ordinary old guy killing time while his wife fixed lunch? What if the Crossroads *was* just a story thought up to make something out of nothing?

The old man reached up, pushed his hat back on his head, and fixed Maz with a set of eyes as ancient and watery as the rivers that ran through the South like arteries to the great heart of the Mississippi.

If the Crossroads was nothing but a story, there was only one way to find out.

"That's a fine guitar you've got there," Maz said. "I'm a guitar player myself."

"That right?"

"I'm pretty good at it, too. Only not as good as I'd like to be."

"Ain't nobody ever that good," the old man said.

"I heard there was someone around here who could help get a person that good, though."

"And who would this someone happen to be, boy?"

"The devil," Maz said, and held his breath.

The old man exploded with a burst of laughter so fierce Maz thought he was going to fall off his stool. His white teeth flashed like tombstones against his dusky skin; the inside of his mouth was as red as a gaping wound.

"Now, 'cuse my lack of manners, boy" he finally managed. "But that's one good laugh you gave an old man."

"So this isn't the place where the devil rides by the Crossroads when the clock strikes midnight?"

"The devil, you say? Lots of folks 'round here go by that name." The old man leaned forward and Maz had to force himself not to step back. There was some strange vibration coming from that withered body, like a downed live wire sending deadly electric pulses out through the ground. "Which devil in particular you lookin' for?"

"The one who knows how to tune a guitar with the fires of hell itself."

"Well, why didn't you just say so, boy? You's looking for the Trickster, then."

"The Trickster?"

"That's right."

"Is the Trickster what the devil's called down here?"

The old man slapped his knee and roared with laughter again. "We's all devils down here, boy. Nothin' but."

"What if there isn't a band? What if it's a solo act?" It would take some doing, but Maz could probably convince them to drop Sweet Tonic and use only his name.

But the old man just snorted in contempt. "Call things what you will, boy, there's *always* a band."

"It's the star players the Trickster wants most, though, right?"

"Often times enough. But check that list of yours again, boy. Plenty of second fiddles on there, plus a whole lot more than don't ever make no lists."

Maz stood there in the baking heat trying to keep the ground from spinning beneath his feet.

"What's the matter, boy? Cat got yer tongue?" The old man leaned back and pulled his hat down over his eyes as if he knew what decision had been made before Maz had even decided it.

"I don't think I can make a deal like that," Maz said.

"That's fine, boy. Never no shortage of hungry young players looking to make a deal."

The rental car seemed very far away, and Maz concentrated on putting one foot in front of the other. He was halfway across the field when the old man's gravel-bed voice stopped him.

"Come on back you ever change your mind, boy—Trickster's always looking to add more musicians to the band!"

Maz turned around to reply, but the old man wasn't there. The only thing left on the sagging porch was the weather-beaten stool and the shadow of where he might have been.

"Man, you got the fire inside tonight!" Ethan said, slamming a cymbal for emphasis.

"Let's hope it's hot enough," Maz said.

The sound check was finished and they were as warmed up as they were ever going to be. Sweet Tonic took the Bowery stage in less than an hour. The only thing to do now was to hang around the dressing room and try not to lose their minds.

As the Delta had receded to a speck in the plane window, Maz had vowed to say a final goodbye to the story that had brought him there in the first place. On the trip back to New York he thought about all the great musicians out there slugging their way toward success. Some made it, most didn't, and more than a few died trying. But every one of them stepped into the ring with only hard work and talent to go against an opponent notorious for throwing all kinds of wild swings and sucker punches. Nobody could rig the outcome in a match like that, not even the Trickster.

When the stage manager stuck his head through the door and said, "You're on," the only tricksters that mattered were the three label reps from Prince Jam records sucking down free drinks at the bar.

That night the band played as if their lives depended on every note of every song. Maz especially worked that guitar and howled out the lyrics as if the devil himself was right on his heels, ready to snatch him up the second he stopped to catch his breath.

The show was the best Sweet Tonic had ever played. Sitting around the dressing room exhausted and elated in equal measure, no one had to ask what those label reps were going to say.

"Me, first thing I'm gonna do is get a big apartment in Cobble Hill," Tito said. "Everybody gonna have their own rooms. No more sleepin' on couches for the Arrieta *familia!*"

"I'm gonna go on the biggest shopping spree you ever saw," Nicki said. "What about you, Maz? You gonna spring all of us for some Dom Perignon at the Palace?"

Before Maz had time to answer the three label reps slid into the room sporting suits that probably cost more than Tito's two paychecks combined.

"Relax, keep comfortable," one of them said. "We just popped in to give our compliments on a very fine show."

"We see a lot of shows from a lot of bands," another suit said. "So those compliments don't come easy."

Maz tried to stay focused on the blur of mutual admiration that floated by on a gallon of freshly-spilled snake-oil, but he was glad when everybody started shaking hands and saying their goodbyes.

"So we'll be hearing from someone at Prince Jam soon?" Maz asked.

The three suits looked at each other. For the first time all night Maz felt that familiar, slow fizz of failure rise up in his gut.

"Well, like I said," the suit reminded him. "You were hot tonight, no doubt about it, but we see a lot of hot bands. What we're really looking for is one with something special—that *thing* that's really gonna take it all the way. You know what I mean?"

Everyone looked at Maz. There was no doubt about which member of the band they were talking to *and* about.

"Yeah, I know what you mean," Maz said.

"Now, Sweet Tonic has another show coming up at, let me see... The Five Note, right?"

"Right."

"Well, how about we catch you then and see how things go—see if we can't get a bit of that somethin' goin' on next time, all right?"

They all shook hands and smiled and back-slapped, and once the suits were gone everybody sat around not knowing what to say.

Tito finally broke the silence. "Anybody want to get some chicken at the Hurry-Curry? I'm starved."

But nobody else was hungry. Most of all, nobody wanted to sit around and share the misery. Soon it was just Maz and Laurid left in the dressing room.

"Still think it's not worth selling your soul for?" Maz asked her. He didn't even bother keeping the bitterness out of his voice.

"Baby, that's just a *story*," Laurid said. "And yeah, I *still* don't think any amount of success is worth selling your soul for, literally or otherwise. We still got a lot, big-time record deal or no."

"A lot isn't enough. We're as good as any band in the city—*better* than most, in fact. But think how it is, Laurid—how some artists just as talented and hard-working as the next guy never make it, while the next guy goes all the way to the top."

"Comes down to luck, I guess. All you can do is hope some comes your way."

"Seems to me you have to make your own luck instead of hopin' some just drops by on its own," Maz said.

"Well, I'm gonna start mine off with a strong drink. Come with me to the Hi-Low?"

"Nah, I need some alone time. I'll catch up with you later."

After she'd gone, Maz sat in the darkened dressing room until the janitor finally locked up for the night. Then he caught a cab to J.F.K. airport and maxed out his credit limit with a red-eye flight to Clarksdale, Mississippi.

Maz was more than ready to make his own luck, and there was a Trickster down South who knew just how to put that kind of sugar in his bowl.

"God-*damn* where's the devil when you need him?" Maz had driven up and down every back road in the county and he still couldn't find the old farmhouse.

It was almost midnight when he drove back to the Crossroads and parked his car right in the middle of the road. He got out and called across the empty fields, but nothing answered back.

"What's the matter, Trickster? You don't need any guitar players right now?"

"You don't have to shout, boy. I can hear you just fine."

Maz spun around and saw the old man standing at the edge of the uneven circle of road, only this time he didn't look so old. The withered body was taller, straighter—not the body of an old man, but a strong, young one. The ancient face was still the same, though, or maybe it was just those black-water eyes. The battered cowboy hat definitely hadn't changed, and he tipped it at Maz in greeting.

The Gibson was thrown across his back like an old-time gunslinger in a Wild West shoot-out.

"I'm here to take that deal we talked about, if it's still on offer," Maz said.

"Deal's always on offer, boy. Only you got to be sure. There ain't no double-dealin' the Trickster."

"I'm sure," Maz said. "Just give the band one break and you can come drag *all* our souls to hell when it's time to pay our dues."

"Hell? Ain't no hell about it, boy. Just this side, that side, and the other. All the same sides, tell you the truth, but only them that's been around a long, long time know how to travel back and forth between 'em just as easy as hoppin' trains."

"And the Trickster is very, very old," Maz whispered.

The old man Maz now understood to be the Trickster stepped closer to him. He smelled like earth—deep and dark as time itself.

"One of the oldest there is, boy."

The Trickster swung the Gibson around front and played a strangely discordant riff in a key Maz couldn't identify. He lifted the strap over his head and handed the guitar to Maz.

"You go on now, boy. Give it all you got, and that Gibson gonna give back the same."

Maz tried to stop his hands from shaking as he grasped the impossibly smooth wooden neck, but it was no use. He ran his trembling fingers across the strings and closed his eyes. It was as if every vibration of every note came from someplace in his soul he'd never even known existed.

The Trickster laughed and clapped his hands. He began dancing a bizarre little jig around the Crossroads.

Maz closed his eyes again, really strumming now. He was about ready to stop when he felt the music break straight out of his skin and travel all the way into the stratosphere and back down again. That feeling was worth a dozen souls, a thousand, even. In the middle of the Crossroads with the hum of the guitar still vibrating through him, Maz knew it was more than worth any price the Trickster wanted him to pay.

For a few years after Sweet Tonic broke big, Maz checked the weather forecast every night they were out on the road. He studied hotel emergency exit plans and forbid anyone who wanted to stay in the band to take so much as an extra aspirin for a headache. When they got their own plane, Maz paid a ridiculous amount to get the best pilot in the business. He made everybody practice the evacuation procedure so many times they almost wished they were back in the tour bus.

But after a while it got easier and easier to forget. Laurid was now "Mrs. Maz," but no fool would ever call one of the world's best bass guitar players anything other than *Ms.* Laurid, thank-you-very-much. Sometimes she teased Maz about "that old Robert Johnson story you used to go on about all the time." Sometimes Maz even started believing that the whole thing *was* just a crazy story, that some old-timer down in the Delta was still having one hell of a laugh about the big city Yankee who thought he'd made a deal with the devil at the Crossroads.

Then he'd get on stage and the music would break straight out of his skin and travel all the way through the roof and into the stratosphere like it still did sometimes when the mood was right and the smell of dark earth was in the air.

When that happened, Maz tried not to look down—it was a long, long way to fall. And somewhere down there was a very old man sitting beside a river even older and darker than time itself.

He was picking a wartime Gibson flat-top, waiting for the rest of the band to show up.

Earth Shall Return Them

The mummified corpse was blackened with time and twisted into a fetal position so severe it was almost spherical, but it was still unmistakably human. However, every time Dr. Rahmano looked at it, he had to remind himself that sometimes "human" was a relative term. He had read the results of the D.N.A. experiments at least a dozen times and the findings were never any less astonishing. His colleagues on the project included some of the best cultural archeologists in the world, and they had been speculating for days about possible explanations.

"Maybe it was a simple attempt to replace missing parts. A head gets lopped off here, an arm goes missing there. Just attach a spare for the burial ceremony and no one's the wiser," Dr. Kupelian offered.

"Or it could be a form of documentation. A literal merging of body parts in order to represent merging families and lines of descent," Dr. Byrne said. A world-renowned expert in the field of ancient burial rites, she was the lead researcher on the project. Taken together, their team represented decades' worth of research, study, and expertise in over a dozen different fields. Dr. Rahmano had enormous respect for every one of them and had listened carefully to all of their theories.

Yet something just didn't feel right about whatever had happened to those corpses.

At first it had seemed like any other archeological find— extraordinary due to the age of the remains, but otherwise unremarkable. Only later, when the test results were in, did things get strange.

Dr. Byrne had called the team together in the research lab. There was an edge to her usual restrained manner that day, and they soon found out the cause.

"The experiments have revealed something a bit unusual about our ancient friends," she told them. "It seems that the corpses are not actually composed of just one set of D.N.A., but rather contain as many as six distinct individual gene patterns."

"Sorry, come again?" they all asked in one form or another.

She looked down at the graphs and charts as if to re-convince herself of their content.

"Put another way," she said, "the corpses are a hybrid of body parts from as many as three, four, sometimes even six different people."

The team had uncovered a dozen corpses so far and had only run tests on three of them. There were more remains scattered throughout the dig site; it was very likely that some of them would also turn out to be composite corpses.

In their typically subtle fashion, the press dubbed the findings "Frankenstein Mummies." Within days, everyone from alien conspiracy theorists to zombie apocalypse preparation teams was abuzz with wild speculations and conjecture.

"Of course there isn't enough left of the remains to tell us *how* the body parts were joined together," Dr. Byrne told the reporters.

"And I'm afraid that even with our most well-informed theories, the more elusive question of 'why' will ultimately remain a mystery."

Dr. Rahmano peered down at the bones. What bizarre rituals had been at work to create the Frankenstein Mummies? What secrets had been buried forever in those ancient graves?

The bones, inscrutable as ever, provided no answers. Whatever secrets they possessed were going to stay buried even though their inhabitants had not. Whatever strange story surrounded them had been lost forever in the ancient mists of unrecorded time.

The small group of men stood in a semi-circle at the edge of the sea. The wind sent the cloaks around their shoulders flapping in all directions like a flock of startled birds. A raven circled overhead in solitary flight. Some of the men took this to be an ill omen. Others thought it was a sign that the spirits would once again defend the island against the invaders from the north.

One man among them, though, cared little about the hidden messages of the spirit world. He was far more concerned about this one. A series of figures had been drawn in the sand at his feet. It was a rough sketch of tomorrow's battle plan, and the terribly lop-sided numbers on each side were the cause of his great troubles.

The heavy gold torc around his neck and the rich green cloak fastened with an intricate clasp signaled the man's noble rank, but no onlooker would have needed such superficial signs. His proud bearing and the deferential attitude of the other men made it clear enough that he was their leader.

"There could be as many as a hundred ships this time," Chief Drustan told his men. "We must be prepared to be outmatched in numbers if not in strength of will."

They were his twelve best warriors. He knew each and every one of them as well as he knew his own children. Some he'd bounced on his knee when they were still babies pulling at his beard, and many were now married with beard-pulling babies of their own. A month ago, Fáelán's wife had given birth to their first child, a girl with the exact same copper-colored curls as her father.

All of Chief Drustan's men trusted him as both a leader and a friend. Yet tomorrow morning he would send most of them to a certain death on the very ground upon which they now stood.

"The spirits of Water and Air will once again come to our aid," one of the men said. "From before time they have protected this island and they will not desert us now."

Chief Drustan sighed and nodded in agreement, for what else could he do? He had wished many times that he shared his people's faith in the powers of the island spirits. Never had he needed it more than when the first ships had arrived from the north. They had been filled with warriors so numerous that the sun glints from their shields and armor had been visible miles from shore. He had to admit that the island spirits had more than proven their worth that day—as the treacherous vessels had drawn closer and closer, the sky had suddenly blackened with clouds. A fierce wind rose from the sea and turned the lashing rain into a frenzied dervish. By the time the storm calmed to a steady rain, every ship in the enemy fleet had been wrecked and lost to the sea.

The clan had thrown a victory feast that lasted three days and nights. The Robed Men had made many sacrifices in gratitude to the spirits, but Chief Drustan had known the invaders would be back.

And even if the spirits once again helped to defeat the invaders, even they could not fight the most powerful enemy of all: Time.

Unlike the men gathered around him so ready to die before they had even truly lived, Chief Drustan was old enough to know that Time was the one foe that could never be beaten. It was followed everywhere by its constant companion, Change, and not even the island, so long forgotten by the world beyond the sea, could escape that all-annihilating duo forever.

If the invaders took the northern shoreline tomorrow, the rest of the island would fall. The women and children had already been moved inland, but it had been a symbolic gesture more than a practical strategy. If the people no longer had hope, the battle was lost already.

Chief Drustan erased the sketch of the battle plan with the toe of his laced leather boot. No schemes or figures could change things now. Tomorrow his men would be outnumbered by warriors far more skilled and better equipped than the simple fishermen and craftsmen who had pledged to join him in defending the island. Chief Drustan's faith was not as strong and sure as his men's, but he would not deny more practical matters of survival like how to use fire or catch the creatures of the land and sea. When they could teach her no more they took her to the hut that had been her home for almost forty turns of the seasons.

She was an old woman now, and those who had taught her were all long dead.

The men were slowly dispersing from the shoreline, but the great chieftain lingered. Earth's heart ached with the knowledge of what he could not yet see. The spirits had told the Robed Men when the ships from the north would arrive, but even the Robed Men had not seen what she had. Like the chieftain, Earth had known the invaders would return. At the first glimpse of the enemy ships with their bows curved like rams' horns and their masts aloft with the flags of past victories, a scar of fear had stricken her skin and rooted downward into her soul.

Something terrible had come to the island in those ships, and the next time it wouldn't be so easily defeated.

She had fasted, burned herbs and incense, and prayed to the spirits for sight. On the seventeenth day, the scrivening stone showed her not a hundred ships but three hundred. She saw the shoreline decorated with the bodies of the fallen; she heard the terrible screams of the dying; she watched the island burn with the fires of a thousand flames that not even the great chieftain would be able to tame.

That's when the old woman had known that a new kind of magic was necessary—a magic as fierce and uncompromising as the enemy itself.

Even from the height of the cliff top she could read the worry in the chieftain's face, could see the heavy weight of his people's fate upon his shoulders. Earth was not of those people, but she loved them as fully as if they were her own children. In a way, they *were* her own children, for they were of the island, and she was the island as much as any form made of flesh and blood could be. She would fight for her children as fiercely as any mother, and she would die for them, too.

But not before she had secured a promise from the spirit which so long ago had claimed her as its own.

The first time the invaders had been defeated by Water and Air. She laughed at the way those two were bound to each other like squabbling, affectionate siblings. They were both mercurial, elusive spirits, but far less so than Fire. That one was perhaps the most powerful of all the elementals, and so the most dangerous. Fire made no promises and honored no oaths, not even to its Chosen One.

Water and Air had done their part, and now they were tired. She had already seen the way Fire looked hungrily at the shoreline, ready to be unleashed by the chaos and madness of men. It was up to her alone to save the island from the invaders intent upon destroying it.

But Earth's powers were more subtle than her companions. Unlike Fire, Water, and Air, her gifts were slower to arrive, and sometimes more difficult to see. Earth was exactly as she seemed—

would not try to stop those who wished to go, but he knew that most would stay and fight even in the face of certain death.

There was little time to spare, but he ordered the Chosen One to be buried at the foot of the cliffs that had sustained her for so long. The boy had run to fetch one of the Robed Men and they performed a ceremony in her honor. It wasn't enough for one as sacred as she, but for now it was all they could offer.

The first masts with their frightful flags assaulting the air had already been spotted on the horizon.

Not one man made a sound as the vessels came into view, but they knew that even Chief Drustan was taken aback by the ships so numerous they seemed to cover the sea—and each one filled with warriors eager to claim their lost conquest.

If Earth had already forsaken them, it seemed that Water and Air would do the same. The sky was a perfect, cloudless blue, the sea a carpet of gentle waves.

The first line of warriors held fast as the vessels came to ground and gorged forth their blood-thirsty contents, but the islanders were no match for their invaders. Soon the shoreline was a blur of running men and terrified horses; blades flashed through the air like lightning and shields glinted in the rising sun; the screams of the dying formed an endless dirge with the crashing waves and cries of the circling ravens.

Chief Drustan had taken a spear in the side. His men dragged him to shelter at the far end of the shoreline where he lay with the blood seeping through his already drenched tunic. There were not many islanders left standing among the invaders. Most had been reduced to heaps of flesh and scattered limbs. They were fighting the enemy ten to one now and would not last the afternoon. Chief Drustan thanked the spirits for allowing him to live and die on the island, and prayed that his people would not suffer.

He had made his peace and was preparing to cross over to the Other Side when something caught his eye:

Earth shall—

The words that had been found scrawled into the sand by the Chosen One's body were still visible. Chief Drustan took great comfort in the thought that he would die in the same place where she had fallen. He reached toward the words and as his fingers touched the sand the letters began to fill with crimson liquid that came from no sea or river he'd ever known. Chief Drustan watched as the rest of the message revealed itself as if written by some unseen hand:

Earth shall return them.

The guard next to him cried out and pointed toward the shoreline.

"By all that is sacred, Chief, what sorcery is this?"

Chief Drustan struggled to a seated position, but what he saw almost sent him back to the sand in a faint. It was against all he knew of the laws of both this world and the Other Side, but he could have sworn that the bodies of the fallen were rising from the ground to once again take up their swords against the invaders.

At dusk the people gathered at the warriors' burial ground to lay the monument. It was a simple round river stone, for the rituals of the island people were neither elaborate nor excessive.

Chief Drustan knelt on the fresh mound and bowed his head. The Robed Men chanted and the people gave thanks to the spirits of the island. At last Chief Drustan placed the stone upon the mound. The Master Engraver had inscribed its smooth surface with the following words:

Earth Shall Return Them

"Here rest our finest warriors," Chief Drustan said. "Tales of their heroic deeds will spread across the sea and turn enemies from our shores for many generations to come. For this we thank the spirits of the island, and most of all Earth, who gave us back these warriors in our time of need. Thus back to the Earth we now return them."

He turned to face the sea and his voice hardened against the wind.

"And for those generations not yet dreamed of who may one day uncover these bones, this stone will remind them that as long as this island remains, those who honor its spirits shall also remain!"

The people gazed at the stone and then out across the vast and mysterious sea. They could not know that by the time the generations not yet dreamed of uncovered the bones, the inscription would have been long ago erased by time, the stone itself returned to the waters from which it came. They could not know that by then most people would have forgotten the spirits of the island, the great powers of Earth,

Air, Water, and Fire reduced to little more than tools to manipulate and exploit.

But the island which existed long before mankind and shall exist long after mankind has gone knows that there are always some who remember. And so the spirits remain, and wait, ready to once again whisper their ancient secrets into the ears of those who know how to listen.

In fact, that awareness might have been what started the whole problem in the first place.

Zach set the crosshairs and waited for the alchemical moment when the map in front of him, the image in his head, and pure, blind instinct came together just right. That combination had made Zach one of the most accurate fire watchers in Coconino, if not the entire state of Arizona.

Not bad for a guy nobody thought could even make it into the fire station let alone handle himself once he got there.

This sighting would be his thirty-third so far this season. Last month, a lightning fire in the Tonto National Forest had traveled over twenty miles in one afternoon. By the time it was contained, almost a hundred thousand acres had been turned to blackened ash and a housing development had been leveled. Three people had lost their lives, including two firefighters.

"Got it!" Zach said as the crosshairs found their target. He entered the numbers into the GPS coordinator and was about to call it in when the voices came. They were the same whispery, disjointed voices that had come to him three months ago when he'd first started the job. They sounded like a thousand voices all swirled and blended together, separate yet somehow the same—voices like the thousand small flames that feed one raging wildfire.

Let it burn, the voices said.

For three months, Zach had been fighting their seductive promises.

Let it be cleansed, let it be reborn anew. Let creation come from destruction, as all life must come from death.

Let it burn.

For three months, Zach had stopped the flames. But each time he'd wondered more and more about those fiery promises. Each time the allure of those voices grew stronger.

All began with fire, so must all return, the voices reassured him. *Let it burn.*

The call-in radio was still in his hand. The plume of smoke was bigger now, rising skyward. The winds were high today, and Zach knew that conditions were perfect for the most dreaded and most fascinating of all fire phenomena: the fire whirl.

"Around here we call them fire devils, 'cause that's exactly what they are—devils straight from hell itself," his boss had told him. "Things are like mini tornadoes of spinning flame. I once saw a fire devil more than five hundred feet in diameter rip a sixteen-inch limb off an oak tree like it was a twig."

Since then Zach had learned all he could about these mysterious, deadly devils. He knew that when the air temperature and currents are just right, a spinning column of hot air and gases rises into a vortex of flame. He'd found out that larger fire whorls can generate winds of more than eighty miles per hour. He'd read about how the 1923 Great Kantō earthquake in Japan had ignited a fire that produced a gigantic fire whirl. Thirty-eight thousand people had been killed in less than fifteen minutes. Zach knew as surely as he'd ever known anything in his saw the skin compress, but he might as well have been pressing on someone else's body, because his didn't feel a thing. Of course Zach knew by then that he had no sensation left below the waist, but being totally responsible for those pale, atrophied, and utterly useless legs for the first time had filled him with a kind of dread he could neither analyze nor explain.

There had been a lot to get used to after waking up in that hospital bed: the catheter tubes he had to stick in his dick to drain the piss out; the fact that even when he did manage to get a woman to come home with him he had to take a pill just to get that same dick to function even halfway properly; the helplessness of needing lifted or carried into places even a child could go; always looking up at a world that more often than not chose to look away.

But a person can get used to almost anything if he's determined enough, and Zach had never been short on determination. Even so, almost two years later it still threw him sometimes to look down and wonder how those two dead legs had gotten attached to his body. Half of his anatomy no longer belonged to him, yet there it was, dragging around after him like a Siamese zombie twin permanently attached at the waist.

For a long time his dream-self still walked. Somewhere around the one year mark, the chair showed up for the first time. Once he had dreamed that he was flying, but not like a bird or an airplane. It had been more like floating—more like burning embers traveling through the air like infinite little fire spawn determined to finish their progenitor's mission.

His first bed sore had been the unlikely source leading him back to fire. It was on the back of his upper thigh, and he wouldn't have even known it was there if Lisa hadn't spotted it.

"It looks really painful, Zach," she told him.

"Lucky I can't feel it then. Hold the mirror up and let me see."

"Why do you want to see a nasty sore?"

"Because I'm gross that way. Come on, hold the mirror up."

The sore was about the size of a quarter, red and raw and livid.

"You're right," Zach said. "It does look painful. It's like someone burned me with a lit cigar just for not moving around enough."

That image had no doubt been at the back of his mind the night in the bar when he'd had too many beers and too much attitude from the group of jackasses that kept bumping his chair around like he was part of the furniture.

"Hey, buddy, can you move that thing out of the way?" one of them finally said. "It's getting pretty crowded up here."

What happened next surprised Zach even more than the jackasses.

"I'd love to move, buddy, but you see, I've got a little problem with that," Zach said. "Here, I'll show you just how much of a problem I have." He reached up, took the lit cigarette out of the guy's hand, and the entrance, and best of all for Zach, it was equipped with a small ramp to wheel in equipment and supplies.

"Seems as if this station was built just for someone in your position," his boss told him on his first day of training. "That is to say, you being in the wheelchair and, uh…"

"Paraplegic," Zach offered.

"Right! Anyway, most people can't stand the loneliness, but if you're a solitary type of man like I am, it's a damn near perfect job."

Zach was a solitary type of man, and it was a damn near perfect job, though he'd almost backed out before he'd even started. The problem had been the ramp. It had been made for supply carts pushed from behind, not a wheelchair pushed by the guy sitting in it, and Zach could see right away that it was too short and too steep. But the only way he was getting into that station was up that ramp. His boss had already started up, and Zach strained every muscle he had to follow him.

By the time he reached the top he was covered in sweat and his arms felt like someone had beaten them with a steel pipe. His boss gave him a sideways look that contained none of his former good humor.

"Say, the Forest Service has plenty of desk positions that might be easier—"

"No, no," Zach had laughed, easy and breezy as can be. "It's just the air's a little thinner up here than what I'm used to."

"Oh! Right. That does take some getting used to. Now let me show you the equipment you'll be using. All state of the art, but I'm telling you, a good set of eyes is still the best prevention around."

Even though Zach could barely lift his arms over his head the next morning, for the rest of his two week training he had taken that ramp as if he were strolling through a park. His boss had hinted around that he could put in a request for funds to lengthen it, but by that time Zach would have drug himself up the damn thing on his belly rather than let it get the better of him. He still struggled with that ramp every morning, but a person gets used to anything if he's determined enough. Besides, he had learned long ago that punishing his body helped keep his brain at bay, and physical pain was the far more preferable kind.

That was another thing he liked about the job—scanning out over the forest with nothing but the hawks and golden eagles for company, his mind drifted into blankness.

Somewhere in that blankness, though, the voices had found him.

They came to him during his first fire. A blaze over at Eagle Rock had been sweeping its way through the upper half of the park, and Zack had his eye on a pine that was quickly threatening to turn into a giant firecracker. Embers launched from the top of a tree fire could sometimes reach two and half times the height of the tree and start new fires up to three miles away. Zack's district was on high alert for flash points.

thought about; fire was all that mattered. And more than anything else, Zach wanted to see it unleashed, finally set free from its boundaries.

For three months he had been fighting the voices. But there comes a time when even the most determined person gets tired of fighting.

Zach reached the service road near the Mount Elden tree line just as the blaze was creeping its way up the side of the canyon. Once it reached the top, it would find plenty more to feed on than dry brush. If it reached the tree line, there would be no stopping it.

He abandoned his car at the top of a service road and maneuvered his chair as close to the edge of the canyon as he could get. Even with his off-road mountain tires, he would never make it down the steep, rocky incline. But all he needed now was to wait. The air was already thick with acrid smoke and parched from the heat of the spreading flames.

One well-formed fire devil would be enough to jump the canyon edge. Zach knew it was coming. He could *feel* the wind and fire and embers coming together in the terrible creation of destruction.

The smoke made it difficult to swallow now. He watched the flames devour a sage bush, and as the wind took the burning leaves and debris, he saw it: a small fire devil was whirling to life at the base of the canyon.

Soon the fire would be free, and no one would be able to stop it.

A golden eagle wheeled overhead, cawing out a frantic warning. The heat rose out of the canyon and scorched Zach's already parched throat. The pine trees shimmered in the heat like ancient specters. A doe bolted out of the tree line followed by a struggling fawn still small enough to be wearing spots. Zach could tell already that it would never be able to keep up with its mother.

Smoke blinded his eyes and filled his mouth with the taste of burning.

The taste was bitter and black.

The fire whorl had taken shape and was gaining speed. Zach watched in equal parts fascination and horror as it jumped a dried stream bed and began to climb the canyon wall. The fire was a raging orgy of dancing flames now, powerful and wild and beautiful. But it was beautiful only *before* its aftermath, powerful only *before* the consequences it could neither predict nor control. In the haze of smoke, Zach now saw beyond the fire and into the ashes that would remain—unchecked beauty turned to ruin; power uncontained rendered powerless.

Like a man waking from a terrible dream only to realize he's been awake all along, Zach reached for his phone.

"Please let me get through," he pleaded. "Please let me remember the coordinates."

One thing, at least, he thought before the smoke overtook him. *I finally did come face-to-face with a fire devil.*

The Mirror Tells a Different Tale

My first one was for assault and battery. In those days the station didn't have one-way mirrors yet, so there was nothing separating the witness and the suspects. The cops tried to keep the witnesses kind of shadowed so that we couldn't see them too well, but you can imagine how well that worked out. I often wondered how many of those witnesses chickened out at the end just from worrying how many of us were sitting up there studying them the same way they were studying us.

Most of them studied us as carefully as if life and death depended on it. And sometimes, it did.

It seems kind of strange now that I never wondered why Detective James Brody just called me up out of the blue one day asking if I'd be willing to come down to the station and participate in a police line-up. I'd never been arrested or had anything to do with the police before in my life. But I was still young then, and even more stupid than I am now. Not to mention a whole lot more broke. Even though volunteers only got a token payment for their time and trouble, in those days I needed all the extra I could get.

If I'd have known the kind of price I was going to pay, though, I might have just looked for a second job instead.

I've been through dozens of line-ups by now, but I remember that first one just as if it happened yesterday. About a dozen of us sat around in a room drinking bitter coffee out of paper cups, and it took me a while to realize that we all looked pretty much alike: Caucasian;

target. But then again maybe this suspect was crafty enough to know that most guilty men would never put themselves front and center, so wouldn't that actually be the safest place for a guilty man to be?

I was in position number seven, which I'd always considered my lucky number. Some crazy luck I turned out to have.

The witness stood there looking at each of us long and hard. I did my best to play the dummy, but then he fixed his eyes right on me, and that's when things started getting really strange. First my stomach knotted up, and then a film of sweat broke out on my upper lip just as if I was the one who had hit Mr. High-Flown Hair instead of the guy seated two doors down.

I told myself it was natural to feel guilty sitting in a police line-up with the witness staring daggers into you. But it was more than that. As I tried like hell to keep from jiggling my leg and fidgeting, I felt as if I really *had* committed the crime. I could almost hear the *thwack* of my fist on High-Flown's head, could almost feel the hard knuckle punch against bone.

Apart from a few playground scuffles, I'd never once hit a man in my life.

The witness moved on to the next person and kept going down the line. But eventually he ended up back at position number seven. He stared hard at me, and I stared hard back at him. Then I did something that could have gotten me into the kind of trouble the police sergeant had warned us about. I held his gaze for just long enough, and then I swallowed hard and looked away. It was subtle, but it was enough.

The witness made a motion to the sergeant in charge.

"Can you make an identification?" the sergeant asked.

"Yes," the witness said.

"Are you absolutely certain that you can identify the person that assaulted you on the evening in question?"

"Yes," he said, this time even more firmly.

"Which one was it?"

"Number seven," he said, pointing straight at me.

Sure enough, my mouth went dry and my shoulders slumped just as if I'd been caught. Somebody down the line snickered, and the witness was led out of the room. As I got up to go collect my payment, I noticed that the suspect was grinning.

I didn't get another call from Detective Brody for another six months or so, and by that time I'd pretty much forgotten about the whole thing. But I still needed the money, so I went down to the station and sat there as the make-up lady painted fake mustaches on all of us just like the suspect's thin little lip-rug.

When they brought the witness in to check us out, I didn't go as far as I had the first time, but that same sense of defiance came over me just the same. He walked up and down the line five times before finally pausing in front of my number. I couldn't stop myself from stiffening just a little and casting my eyes down just a bit too quickly. It was an arson case this time, and as I sat there with the sweat running down my

When I got the call from Detective Brody it had been a long spell since my last line-up. I was married myself by then, with a kid about ready to start high school. I didn't need the money anymore, and I was too busy to waste half an afternoon sitting around a police station. And to tell you the truth, by that time the whole thing had started to get to me a little. I'd started having these dreams, see, where I was actually there at the crime scene. And every single time, I was the one committing the crime.

To this day I still don't know what made me go down for the Shuy case. Brody left three messages in two days, so I knew it had to be something big. Maybe I just wanted to have something to tell the guys down at O'Connell's on Saturday night. True as that may have been, I now know something else was at work—Detective Brody wasn't going to take any chances with this one.

I took my position in the line-up that day without any real idea one way or the other about Shuy's guilt. I only knew that every time I looked at those pictures of his wife and three kids, I got a little sick inside. It was up to a jury to decide if Shuy was guilty or innocent, but this time I wasn't going to interfere with that process even one little bit. Not this time, with those faces staring at me every time I turned on the T.V. or computer. I knew I could never survive the kind of dreams that would come out of this one.

They led Shuy in and he stood there with his head bowed and his hands clasped in front of him like they'd already slapped the cuffs on him. He looked just like he did in all of the pictures from the news—a non-descript middle-aged guy with a pot belly and a fast-receding hairline.

A blonde lady in an expensive-looking suit gave him the thumbs-up sign before the sergeant shooed everyone else out of the room and closed the door. I wondered if she was his lawyer or something else.

Sure enough, Shuy chose position number five—dead center like the bull's-eye of a target.

I forced myself to think of my body like a piece of stone, incapable of even the slightest movement. I imagined being somewhere really nice, maybe lying on a tropical beach or sitting beside a cool mountain stream—anything to keep from thinking about the witness moving up and down on the other side of that glass.

The one way mirror was supposed to block out everything, and for the most part it worked just fine. But if you knew what you were looking at, you could still catch the shadows that meant people were moving around on the other side.

A dark spot shifted across the glass and then paused in front of each one of us. It repeated this process seven times, each more slowly than the last. Then the shadow stopped at my number.

I felt the sweat break out on my upper lip. It took everything in my power not to fidget, but I knew the more desperate I tried to stay calm, the more desperate I probably looked. I thought about jumping up and shouting, "It's not me, it's not me!" Let them charge me with suddenly he looked a whole lot friendlier. He waved the cop away and offered me his hand.

"I'm Detective Higgs. The desk sergeant wasn't having you on—Detective Brody doesn't work here anymore. But I knew him when he did."

It may sound lousy, but I'll admit I was relieved they'd caught on to Brody before I had to get involved. It was weird that no one seemed to have heard of him, but maybe he'd been working undercover or something. As long as he wasn't rigging cases anymore, I didn't care one way or the other.

"So he'll be removed from the force? Maybe even charged with something?"

Detective Higgs wrinkled his forehead and gave me a strange look. "Pardon me?"

"Detective Brody," I reminded him. "You said he got fired, and I'm just wondering if anything else is going to happen to him."

"I didn't say he got fired," the detective corrected me. "I said he didn't work here anymore. He hasn't worked here for a long time now, and I don't think much of anything is going to happen to him anymore."

"I don't understand."

"Detective Brody is dead. He's been dead for almost twenty years now."

You can just imagine me standing there with my mouth hanging down to the floor and my eyes bulging out of my head like some cartoon character. I sputtered out some kind of protest, but what was there to say? Detective Higgs must have felt sorry for the poor fool looking like he was about ready to have a heart attack right there on the spot, because he gestured for me to follow him over to a wall filled with photographs of police officers in black wooden frames.

"This is our Wall of Honor," he told me. "These are all of the police men and women who have given their lives in the line of duty."

He pointed to a picture high up along the left side of the wall. "That's Detective James Brody."

I stared up at a big man with a jovial smile and fleshy, jolly-looking cheeks to go with it. He looked like a rough-around-the-edges version of the Santa Clauses you saw on the cover of greeting cards—only this Santa had a look in his eyes that said you better not even *think* of trying to pull a fast one with his Naughty-and-Nice list.

"Technically a suicide isn't getting killed in the line of duty," Detective Higgs said. "But there are more than one ways to give your life to this job."

"Suicide?" I was still trying to get my head around the fact that I'd been getting phone calls from a dead man for the past eighteen years.

"That's right. Brody was a good man and a good cop, but sometimes those are the ones who get hit the hardest. He spent five years working a double homicide case. Almost wrecked his marriage and his health, but in the end he helped put the guy on death row. This was back in the days when forensics was only just getting started. Back then

Lucky 13

Iva waited a long time before she made her move. They'd finished the last of the turtle yesterday and no one had spotted a flying fish in days. Arms up and out, crawling on her belly one crab-leg at a time, she made one last hard-fast *lunge*. But the seagull proved faster, and in one swoop of wings it was gone.

The motion set the boat rocking like a sea-sick cradle, and now everyone was wide awake. This morning, the bitter taste of the lost gull was the only thing to fill their mouths.

"The grown-ups will find us soon," Justin whispered, more to himself than any of the others. He took off his glasses and tried to wipe the remaining lens clean with what remained of his shirt, but it was no use. He hadn't wanted to wear the safety strap that made him look like a total dork, but now he was glad his mom had insisted—without it his glasses would have been lost at sea along with everything else. As it was, one lens had been broken in the wreck, leaving him squinting like a pirate with a reverse-purpose eye patch. Maybe a parrot would fly in and sit on his shoulder. If it did, Iva would probably want to eat it.

"I'd give anything for a cheeseburger right now," Bennie said. But then he saw something that made him lose his appetite altogether, a rare feat even when he wasn't half-starved to death. "Gross, look at Ethel's *legs*!"

Three more days came and went without rain. Their tongues began to swell and their throats sealed shut so that it was almost impossible to swallow. Crouched against the sides of the boat to escape the tormenting noonday sun, they stared at each other with hollowed out eyes and waited.

As the sea water crept through the hole in the boat and pooled around their feet like a salty promise of things to come, the idea that they'd been cursed began to sprout like a desperate seed poking its way out of otherwise barren soil. Even Judith was starting to think that maybe Justin was on to something with his unlucky thirteen idea. How else to explain why they hadn't been rescued already? Or why the boat was leaking and they couldn't catch anything to eat… and now it wasn't even *raining* any more.

"I once heard about this lady who was the thirteenth daughter in the family, born on the thirteenth day of the month," Mattie said. She'd never really heard of any such lady, but she was hoping to catch Judith's attention now that their options were looking grim. "She got killed in a freak accident when a bus went over the curb and flattened her. And guess what the first two numbers of the license plate where? Thirteen."

"Bull!"

"Yeah, right!"

But the protests were feebler this time, and something primal stirred to life within the strongest ones, those lucky few most favored to survive by some ancient alchemy of D.N.A. and fate.

"What if it's true? What if we *are* cursed?" some of them whispered once the evening chill had started its nightly assault on their bones.

"There's no such thing as curses."

"But let's say there is—then it's bad luck as long as there's thirteen of us. Which means we won't get rescued..."

"Until—"

"Unless—"

The last of the rain water was gone when Rudy showed them the gouges he'd been making in the side of the boat with his pocket knife. He guarded that knife with his life and never let anyone else touch it even though it meant he had to skin all of the fish and turtles himself.

"I've been keeping track since the start," Rudy said. "Tomorrow makes thirteen days."

No one said anything until Bonnie, the youngest and so least prone to lie, finally spoke up. "Does that mean we're all going to die tomorrow?"

Everyone shouted her down for being a "cry baby" and a "whiner." But by the time the sun disappeared over the flat line horizon, thirteen sets of eyes in thirteen hunger-shrunken skulls stared into a now certain watery grave, and the primal-seed sprang to full form.

That night Judith crouched down next to Marcus and waited until the others had drifted into the fits and starts of unconsciousness that passed for sleep.

"If we get rid of one person, we'll break the curse," she said.

was a trick of light—they were way off course from the normal shipping routes, and he'd only cut through such isolated waters to shave a few days off their schedule. But he checked the binoculars again and sure enough, there it was.

"Lower a lifeboat, starboard! And make it quick, already!"

The captain got them back on course as fast as possible, but the rescue had caused the crew to forget all about their deadlines.

"Miracle is what I call it. Out there hangin' onto a piece of wreckage for who knows how long."

"Wouldn't have been much longer, I can tell you that. No ships comin' through here any time soon. Not with that storm movin' in."

"Even with the storm, I would've kept looking if there'd of been any other survivors," the captain assured them. "But the poor little bugger said he was the only one left."

"*Lucky* little bugger's more like it. If the sun wouldn't have hit them broken glasses of his and thrown that beacon of light up, I'd never have spotted him."

"Yep, that's one lucky fellow if ever I saw one," they all agreed.

In an upstairs cabin beneath a thick, warm blanket, Justin slept soundlessly, his broken glasses with the safety strap laid carefully on the table beside him.

13

She looked up past the buildings and billboards and scanned the skies. Her mother had loved to watch birds from their deck.

"Helen, come out here and look at all of this bird shit," her father would say. "Bird shit everywhere, on the chairs, the steps—look at these piles wherever they sit!"

"Perch."

"What?"

"Birds don't sit. They perch."

"Well, whatever they do, they must shit the whole time they're doing it!" her father would roar. But her mother would just smile, and the bird feeders would stay.

Twenty years ago, she had come home from school, flopped on the couch, and turned on the TV just like she did every other day. The after-school special had just started, and she felt the hazy drift of sleep coming on when something crossed the deck, flicking the room into shadow. She sat up to investigate and saw a golden-brown hawk settle on the porch railing less than four feet away. She went to the screen door expecting it to fly, but it stayed put even after she was right in front of it.

"You're kind of far from home, fellow."

There were plenty of hawks in the San Gabriel mountains where she and her friends went hiking sometimes, but she had never seen one this far in. It stared at her, fierce and secret and knowing. She took a step back.

"And what can I do for you?"

Its *caw-caw-caw* of an answer caused the cat to flee under the couch in terror and Elle to retreat from the screen door. But it kept up the racket, and she edged forward to see what was wrong with it. The hawk went silent, locking her in its gaze. She should probably shoo it away—what if it had rabies or something? But she couldn't break the fairy tale spell of its golden eyes. It stayed still a moment longer before shrieking one last time, and then in one great flap of wings, it was gone.

Wait till she told her mom—talk about bird shit! And then the phone rang and just like that, a perfectly ordinary Friday afternoon became the day when everything collapsed, when nothing would ever go back together in quite the same way. It was someone from her mom's job, and at first Elle couldn't put the words together, couldn't figure out how they related to her. Everything slowed, as if she had been plunged into freezing water, and for some reason, it was impossible to put down the phone, to place one foot in front of the other and answer the front door, to form words and make them come out of her mouth.

Only years later did Elle realize how brave her neighbor had been to tell her the truth.

"Honey, your mom has been shot. I'm sorry, but your mom is dead."

Until that moment, Elle had only known death in passing—someone's grandparent or a car wreck, the occasional premature heart attack or fatal disease. But on June 17, 1989, death stepped forward and fully introduced itself, shook her hand and whispered its secret, terrible name into her ear: *Never Again*.

She had not really believed in death. She knew that her parents would die someday, and she would, too—everyone did. But knowing a thing and believing it are two entirely different things, and who believes in his or her own death? Afterward, in the streets, at restaurants and shopping malls, Elle would look at people drinking coffee or going about their business, and she would know that each and every one of them would die—*must* die. And yet the amazing thing was that none of them seemed to understand this to be so.

She forgot about the hawk in the bewildering chaos of funeral, police, trial, the steady forward-march of routine. But months later when she came upon her mother's death certificate, she reconstructed the timeline: shot at 3:52 p.m., fatal hemorrhaging within minutes. Time of death approximately four o'clock on a Friday afternoon, when a backyard bird enthusiast or daydreaming kid might have spotted an unlikely golden-brown hawk cruising low in an otherwise perfectly ordinary suburban sky.

Ever since then, Elle watched for hawks everywhere. She still saw them while hiking the canyons or driving through the hills, and sometimes they turned up in unexpected places: a freeway sign on the 101; the ledge of a seedy motel on Ivar Avenue, of all places. But she'd never again felt the kind of connection that she'd had on that Friday afternoon, and with each passing year, she saw fewer and fewer hawks no matter how hard she searched for them.

She shifted position and resisted the urge to check the time. Just out of college, Elle had dated a science teacher named Rick who at two and a half years still qualified as her longest relationship, not counting Gary. Rick had considered Elle's graveyard ritual unhealthy. He used to tell her about the stages of grief as if they were one of the scientific theories he taught to bored teenagers every day. They had argued about it, one of those "relationship will never last" warning signs that she'd chosen to ignore. But that had been over ten years ago, and Elle was beginning to wonder if old Rick had been right. Maybe a part of her had stopped believing in the hawks, and that's why she couldn't find them anymore. Or maybe they had stopped finding her.

She closed her eyes and pressed her hands against the ground.

"Where are you, Mom? Are you out there somewhere?" Elle whispered to the silent earth. "Can you hear me? *Can you give me some kind of a sign?*"

A vibration shot through her and she cried out, jumped to her feet—and then cursed her foolishness. She had forgotten to turn off her phone again.

It was Sam Forsythe, her agent. When Elle had started looking for an agent, she had found in Sam a kindred spirit: smart, ambitious enough, but with a reflectiveness, a distractibility that meant he was never going to cross the corporate finish line first. And maybe that's why he had taken her on, as well—they had sized each other up and found a perfect fit. Sam had helped Elle get her first contract at Greene Line Publishing after her articles about the Crazy Girl Killer, a psycho who had stalked strippers at the infamous club on La Brea. The media had gone wild for the case: strippers, grisly murders, and a perpetrator who turned out to be a former child actor who had once played a character with the nickname "Chop-Chop."

The book offers started coming in before Chop-Chop had even broken in his prison uniform, and Elle's career as a "true crime writer" had begun. Her last book, about a physician in Pennsylvania who killed his terminally ill patients and buried them in the garden of his country home, was her fifth. Crime, it seemed, was steady business.

She waited until she'd cleared the gates before calling back; taking a call in a cemetery felt creepy even by L.A. standards.

"This is it, Elle. The big one."

"You always say that, Sam. How about 'This is it, Elle. The medium one.' Or even 'the downright small but it pays the bills' one."

"Oh, no. Not this time. Greene Line has got a big one for you, and I mean a *really* big one. Really big." Sam was practically panting.

"OK, Sam, I'll play. Which homicidal maniac do I get to spend the next six months with this time?" Elle waited, knowing Sam wouldn't be able to resist a dramatic pause.

"Eliot Kingman."

She took the phone from her ear and gaped at it in cartoon character astonishment.

"Elle, are you there? I knew it! I knew you wouldn't believe it. This one is going to mean movie deals, TV specials, who knows what all—we have to work the contract really well on this one, and—"

"Sam, wait a minute, slow down. Why is Greene Line giving me such a big story? What's the catch?"

"There you go. The doubter. Because you're good, how about that's why? And because—and this is how I know we're going to negotiate the hell out of that contract—because

Kingman himself contacted Greene Line about the book and *specifically asked for you*."

"Why would Kingman ask for me?"

"Why did Kingman stab some poor schlep through the heart for no apparent reason when he's a gazillionaire movie producer? You can't ask why about something like that—just thank the gods of Hollywood, whatever publicity-starved has-beens they may be."

It was true that this was huge; Eliot Kingman had been one of the biggest names in Hollywood. Rumors had circulated for years about his erratic behavior and penchant for dark hobbies, so when one of his assistants turned up dead at his mansion one day, no one in the industry had been all that surprised. What *had* been a surprise was that Kingman had been charged and eventually convicted for the crime. After a typical L.A. circus trial that had included everything from a necromancer on the stand to Kingman's newly minted wife being removed from the courtroom for drug possession, Kingman had gone from a multimillion-dollar estate in Malibu to the California Department of Corrections for nineteen years to life.

Back in her apartment, Elle closed the blinds against the city. In the days when she had been living paycheck to paycheck, she had taken a one-bedroom apartment in a building at the wrong end of Sunset called The Bradbury, a gone to seed relic from the 1940s Golden Era still holding ground against Hollywood's perpetual attempts to reinvent itself. The rent had risen ridiculously ever since the Boulevard had replaced its rundown T-shirt and sex shops with an upscale mall and movie theater, and for a while Elle had gone to look at slick modern apartments with doors that didn't weigh a hundred pounds. But she had finally admitted to herself that she didn't really want to move: The Bradbury, with its down-at-the-heels charm and hints of faded glamour, was like a place out of time, and that suited her just fine. Whenever she stepped into the ancient elevator with its scrollwork gate and tattered velvet wallpaper, she felt like a character in a noir film, maybe the femme fatale with a dangerous secret and a heart of gold.

But instead of a dashing, hard-boiled dick in a fedora, all that awaited her were two hungry cats.

"Hey, greedy little great-beings, can you at least wait until I'm in the door?"

They indicated that they could not, and after taking care of the most important members of the household, Elle rummaged for her own dinner. All that turned up was a container of stale-looking rice and shriveled edamame beans.

"I've got to start getting out more," she told the cats, who couldn't have cared less. She ate standing at the kitchen counter before grabbing a Dogfish Head Pale Ale and settling down in front of the computer. She started with Kingman's much publicized arrest.

Tuesday, February 4, 2007

Malibu, Calif.—Legendary movie producer Eliot Kingman was arrested Monday for investigation of homicide after the body of a man was found at his home, authorities said.

Kingman, 52, was arrested at his estate around 3 a.m. in this wealthy oceanside community about 40 miles northwest of downtown Los Angeles.

The police responded to an anonymous call and discovered the body of a white, adult male, a police spokesman reported. The man had been stabbed and was pronounced dead at the scene. An antique dagger was taken into evidence as the possible murder weapon.

Authorities have identified the man as 28-year-old David Klee, employed by Kingman as a research assistant. Police stated that Kingman is the only current suspect in the murder. Bail was set at $1 million.

Kingman wrote and directed hit movies such as *Break of Day* and *Running on Empty,* and has received academy award nominations for his work as both a producer and director. He has two children with his ex-wife, the movie actress Niki Cole. His last movie, the 2005 release *By Night,* was about a vampire searching for acceptance in modern society. Friends and associates say that Kingman's behavior grew increasingly erratic throughout the making of the film.

The film's lead actor Nathan Owen reported that Kingman "would always talk about things like death and the afterlife, and hang around all these freaky people. But I guess that's what really great artists do, you know, get into the work like that."

Elle got another Dogfish and retrieved a notebook from the pile on her desk. Even though she couldn't imagine how writers had managed before Microsoft, when it came to research nothing could replace the tactile pleasure of an old school black-and-white Mead.

She searched the daily updates from the courtroom, remembering what a zoo it had been. Kingman's lawyers had pinned their case on reasonable doubt, starting with Kingman's lack of motive. Then they floated every alternative theory for the murder, from a mysterious third party to the possibility that Klee had killed himself. Despite having the best defense team his considerable amount of money could buy, Kingman himself had proved the most damaging piece of evidence. During initial questioning, he had changed his story several times, which looked even worse once he admitted that after he found Klee's body, he had taken the time not only to remove the dagger but also to wipe it clean before police arrived.

One entry caught her eye for its ludicrous title alone:

Necromancer Takes the Stand

A self-described "necromancer" named Zor Pithador (aka Brian Williams) took the stand today as a witness for the prosecution. Mr. Pithador, who calls himself "a practitioner who summons spirits of divination in order to communicate with the dead," testified that he and Kingman made several visits to the city morgue in an attempt to receive messages from the recently deceased. A spokesperson for the L.A. County Morgue declined to comment about how Kingman and Pithador gained access to the facilities, but said that they are investigating any possible employee misconduct.

In light of the long-standing rules of Los Angeles, where reprieve from any vice can be bought for a high-enough price, no one had ever expected a conviction. But the prosecution had taken every chance to portray Kingman as an unstable man whose growing obsession with death had ended in murder, and Kingman's bizarre behavior had done most of their work for them.

Elle took off her glasses and rubbed her eyes. She wanted to spend some quiet time in her favorite spot, an old recliner that had been in her family for as long as she could remember. It had been reupholstered three times already and the gears were going bad, but she couldn't give it up just yet. Flipped back with the lights off, a Dogfish in hand, and cats in lap—that was Elle's version of meditation, and right now she needed to think. Why would Eliot Kingman want her to write his story? Greene Line had several authors who made the kind of money that someone like Kingman was used to. Elle had a solid enough fan base, but she wasn't even close to being one of Greene Line's top sellers. So Sam's endorsement aside, why would Kingman specifically ask for her?

She had decided to let these questions wait until tomorrow when her phone rang. It was Sam again, who didn't hesitate to call at any hour of the night when either inspiration or anxiety struck, the latter being the much more frequent motivation.

"Get ready to not sleep tonight."

"Sam, I'm already not sleeping because I'm on the phone with you. Is this a sign of things to come until the Kingman contract comes through?"

"Probably, but that's not why I called. It's actually bigger than that."

"Bigger than a contract? What, is Kingman going to give us the scoop on who shot JFK or the whereabouts of the Roswell alien?"

"OK, joke. Laugh all the way to Delano State Prison, in fact."

"What?"

"It turns out Kingman's lawyer has been in touch with Greene Line for over a month now. He wants an interview, and you've already been cleared."

"Seems like Kingman is calling the shots from inside the same way he did on the outside."

"Ain't money grand?"

"We wouldn't know. When's it going to be?" Interviews often produced some great material, but they could be difficult to arrange. So many things could go wrong, from obstinate prison officials and cautious lawyers to interfering family members. The subjects themselves often turned skittish or manipulative from one visit to the next.

"Tomorrow." Sam must have known what was coming.

"You've got to be kidding! I just found out I was even *doing* the Kingman story—I've had *zero* time to prepare!"

"It's a two-hour drive to Delano. Prepare on the way."

"Sam, there's no way I can go in cold like that. Tell Greene Line to reschedule."

"Elle, this is Eliot Kingman. You can't reschedule Eliot Kingman, even in prison. Listen, this is the biggest story of your career. Ace this story and you're set. Seriously."

"You mean *we're* set."

"Well, of course, *we're* set! And since we're in it together, I'll go with you tomorrow and do all the driving so you can prepare. Come on, Elle. We're going to have to do this one a bit differently."

"Which means Kingman's way, right?" When Sam didn't answer, Elle gave in. "OK, you win. But you're driving *and* buying lunch."

She sat watching the deepening shadows of evening before heading back to the computer. Sam hadn't been kidding about that sleepless night.